Relaxing

into

Meditation

Ngakma Nor'dzin

Aro Books WORLDWIDE

2010

Aro Books WORLDWIDE
PO Box 65
Penarth, Vale of Glamorgan, Wales, CF64 1XY

Book design, typography and illustrations
by Ngakma Nor'dzin

Edited by Ngakma Métsal Wangmo and
Ngakpa 'ö-Dzin Tridral

Cover photographs by Ngakpa 'ö-Dzin Tridral
Front cover: South Beach, Tenby, Pembrokeshire

Index created by Rossinna Ippolito
http://indocsindexing.com

First Edition 2010
ISBN: 978-1-898185-17-8 (paperback)
ISBN: 978-1-898185-19-5 (hardback)
ISBN: 978-1-898185-19-2 (ePub)

http://aro-books-worldwide.org/relaxing-into-meditation
Aural material to accompany the text
is available from Aro Books WORLDWIDE
Websites of the Aro Lineage: http://www.aroter.org

This book is dedicated to Thelma
(Rin'dzin Gyür-mèd)
whose openness and kindness were unfailing.

Contents

Contents

List of Practices

List of Illustrations

Acknowledgements

It is with great gratitude that I acknowledge the many students of Community Education, and apprentices and disciples of the Confederate Sanghas of Aro who have helped in the production of this book. Special mention must be made of my husband, Ngakpa 'ö-Dzin, and also of Ngakma Métsal Wangmo, Naljorma Rin'dzin Pamo, and Ngakpa Samten Dorje.

I thank the members of my family who posed for the photographs that were the starting point for most of the line drawings that I created to illustrate this book.

Thank you also to Geshé Damchö Yonten of the Lam Rim Buddhist Centre in Wales, and posthumously to Gétsulma Tsultrim Zangmo for teaching me sutric practices.

With great respect and affection I acknowledge the unceasing support and inspiration of my root teachers, the Dzogchen Lamas Ngak'chang Rinpoche and Khandro Déchen.

Ngakma Nor'dzin Rangjung Pamo
Aro Khalding Tsang, Cardiff, Wales
July 2010

Relaxing

into

Meditation

1

Meditation & Relaxation

A group of sixteen people sit in a circle on plastic schoolroom chairs. Their eyes are closed; their hands rest in their laps. Surrounded by the chaotic decoration of a textiles classroom the group has an atmosphere of stillness. The only sounds are slow and gentle breathing, or the occasional cough. After ten minutes, the group leader silently raises a bell, and—after a pause of a few seconds—strikes a single note with the bell's clanger. The pure sound echoes through the room, gradually dying away. Slowly—as the sound fades—each member of the group begins to stir, opening their eyes, stretching their limbs, and smiling at one another. "Good evening everyone. How has your meditation practice been this week?"

This was a typical scene for the opening of one of my relaxation and meditation classes for several years. School rooms are never entirely satisfactory for teaching practices such as meditation but this textiles classroom was one of the better ones. I offered the class as an attempt to bring the practice of meditation—in particular—to a wider audience.

Meditation is a life skill – like taking exercise or learning how to cook. It is a skill that enables anyone and everyone to live their life more fully and more happily. If everyone meditated for a few minutes every day, the world would be a more peaceful and friendlier place.

When I first taught meditation through my local community education programme, I called the course 'meditation for relaxation'. However I realised quite quickly that this title was misleading. Meditation does ultimately lead to deep mental, emotional and physical relaxation that is beyond ordinary expectation. The practice of meditation however, requires commitment and discipline which is not specifically relaxing *in itself* – certainly not initially. Relaxation could almost be said to be a by-product of meditation and it is perhaps unhelpful to approach it from a desire to be more relaxed. I therefore renamed my class 'Relaxation *and* Meditation' so that I could make a clear distinction between meditation and relaxation and offer both to my students.

When enquiring into people's reasons for joining the class, practically every person in all classes replied that they felt meditation would help them to relax and would help them cope with stress. People want their lives to be more peaceful and therefore more enjoyable. They seek contentment and the ability to retain that sense of contentment whatever is happening in their lives. As I said earlier, although meditation certainly leads to relaxation—ultimate and total relaxation—its practice may not be immediately relaxing.

4

In fact meditation practice can be quite demanding because of the necessity to focus and concentrate. It can also be challenging because the development of greater self-awareness through meditation can be a little disconcerting.

Hence in this book I begin our journey towards discovering *ultimate* relaxation by teaching *relative* relaxation. I begin with relaxation and breathing techniques specifically aimed at creating relaxation of the body and calmness of mind before embarking on meditation practices which may be more demanding.

Through the years that I have taught meditation classes—both as a Buddhist teacher and as a community education tutor—I have found that people expect meditation to be a solution to their problems. This was another common factor that arose amongst many of those attending my classes: a need for relief from exceptional personal circumstances such as illness or bereavement. People attended the class in the hope of finding help with a particular personal problem. A period of life with an unusual degree of stress or difficulty however, may not be the best time to try to begin meditation practice and in such circumstances it will certainly be better to begin with relaxation techniques. It is in fact preferable to have established a degree of stability in one's life and relief from immediate pain—mental, emotional or physical—*before* beginning meditation. Hence I begin this book with relaxation techniques to allow us to arrive at a starting point for meditation.

2

Tense & Relax

Two of the large tables have been pushed back against the side wall of the classroom. On the floor lies a group of people. There is barely enough room for them all to lie down without touching each other. Some lie on yoga mats or camping mats, others on sleeping bags. Following an instruction from the tutor, they all stretch their legs, pointing their toes away from them. After another instruction, they all relax their legs as they breathe out. The relaxation practice continues for about ten minutes, guided by the tutor. She then begins to play a recording of classical music and the group lie there with their eyes closed, breathing slowly and rhythmically. After a few moments the music is accompanied by the sound of gentle snoring.

In most cases it will be best to practise a relaxation technique lying down. We are able to more fully allow our bodies to relax when we are in a supine position. If you are not able to lie on the floor, it is fine to use a firm bed. If you have difficulties lying down, you may still find success, enjoyment and benefit practising these relaxation techniques sitting in a chair.

When practising any relaxation technique it is important to be comfortable and warm, so have something soft to lie on in a warm room. You could put a shawl or blanket over you at the end of the practice if you wish.

Do not push your body beyond its natural range of flexibility. None of the techniques and exercises in this book should be the cause of discomfort. If pain or discomfort arises, stop practising the exercise and if necessary seek medical help.

It will be possible to practise these relaxation exercises from memory once you are familiar with them but the effect will not be quite the same as listening to a guided narration. It is more enjoyable and a deeper state of relaxation will be achieved if you have a guide to talk you through the practice. Please see the information at the front of the book about how to acquire a recording of aural material to accompany this book.

Relaxation technique 1 – *Tense and Relax*

Lie where there is room to extend your arms to the side and above your head without touching anything or anyone.
Wriggle around a little to settle yourself into a comfortable position lying on your back with your arms loosely by your sides.

Begin by bringing your attention to your arms.
Tense your arms, holding them straight and rigid.
Breathe in – and then as you breathe out relax your arms.
Let your arms relax into a natural position at your sides.
Repeat the arm tension and relaxation.

Bring your attention to your hands and clench them into tight fists.
Breathe in – and then as you breathe out relax your hands.
Let your hands soften and relax.
Then stretch your hands so that your fingers are taut, straight and wide
apart. Breathe in – and then as you breathe out relax your hands.

Bring your attention to your shoulders. Bring them forward as if you were
trying to make them touch your chest.
Hold the tension. Breathe in – and then as you breathe out relax.
Then push your shoulders back, lifting your upper body slightly as you try
to bring your shoulder blades together.
Breathe in – and then as you breathe out relax back down onto the mat.
Now lift your shoulders as if trying to make them touch your ears.
Breathe in – and then as you breathe out relax your shoulders.
Let your shoulders lie in a natural position.

Bring your attention to your legs. Tense the whole length of your legs from
the hip to the toe. Hold the tension.
Breathe in – and then as you breathe out relax, letting your legs flop open.
Repeat the leg tension and relaxation.

Bring your attention to your feet and toes. Point your toes towards the floor.
Hold the tension. Breathe in – and then as you breathe out relax.
Let your feet relax.
Now pull your toes up towards the body, feeling the tension along the soles
of the feet.
Breathe in – and then as you breathe out relax your feet and ankles.
Wriggle the legs and toes a little and settle your legs into a natural, relaxed
position with the feet flopping out to the side slightly.

Bring your attention to your stomach muscles.
Tighten your stomach muscles so that your stomach becomes flat and pulled
in. Hold the tension.
Breathe in – and then as you breathe out relax.
Repeat the stomach tension and relaxation.

Bring your attention to your buttocks. Tighten the buttock muscles so that
your lower body lifts up from the mat slightly. Hold the tension.
Breathe in – and then as you breathe out relax.
Repeat the tensing and relaxing of the buttock muscles.

Bring your attention to your head and neck.
Very slowly, roll your head over to the left so that your left ear moves
towards the mat. Breathe in – and then as you breathe out try to take your
head a little bit farther round and your ear closer to the mat.
Slowly bring your head back to a central position.
Very slowly, roll your head over to the right so that your right ear moves
towards the mat. Breathe in – and then as you breathe out try to take your
head a little bit farther round and your ear closer to the mat.
Slowly bring your head back to a central position.
Now tip your head to the left, trying to bring your ear as close to your left
shoulder as possible. Feel the tension along the right side of your neck.
Breathe in – and then as you breathe out try to take your head a little bit
farther down.
Slowly bring your head back to a central position. Now tip your head to
the right, trying to bring your ear as close to your right shoulder as possible.
Feel the tension along the left of your neck. Breathe in – and then as you
breathe out try to take your head a little bit farther.
Slowly bring your head back to a central position.

Gently roll your head upwards so that you feel tension in the area under your chin. Stick your jaw out and bring your lower teeth over the upper lip, increasing the tension below the chin. Breathe in – and then as you breathe out relax your jaw into a natural position.
Slowly bring your head back to a central position.
Now gradually move your chin down towards your chest, feeling the tension in the back of the neck.
Breathe in – and then as you breathe out relax.
Slowly bring your head back to a central position.

Now tighten all the muscles in your face so that your face becomes tense. Hold the tension for a few seconds. Breathe in – and then as you breathe out relax the facial muscles.
Now lift the eyebrows as high as possible. Hold the tension for a few seconds. Breathe in – and then as you breathe out relax the eyebrows.
Now make a huge grin with your mouth. Hold the tension in your face for a few seconds. Breathe in – and then as you breathe out relax your mouth.

Bring your attention to your whole body.
Straighten and tighten the arms and legs, pull in the stomach muscles and tighten your facial muscles so that there is tension throughout your body. Hold the tension for a few seconds. Breathe in – and then as you breathe out let go of all tension throughout the body and relax.
Repeat the tensing of the whole body twice more, relaxing on the out-breath.

Mentally scan through your body, bringing your awareness to all the different parts of your body and check for any remaining little areas of tension. If you find any tension, tense and relax that part of your body a couple more times.

Allow yourself to feel that your body is heavy and sinking into the mat.
Feel that your body is completely relaxed.
Stay in this relaxed position, feeling the heavy warmth of your body for as
long as you can, listening to peaceful music if you wish.

When it is time to end the relaxation session, slowly begin to move.
First of all wriggle your feet and hands a little. Slowly take your arms
above your head and stretch along the length of your body.
Bring your knees up to your chest and hug them with your arms. Rock
from side to side, massaging the lower back.
You may find that you release a big yawn or a sigh. Take your time to
prepare for sitting up and standing up. Do not rush it.
If you sit up or stand up too quickly you may find that you are
light-headed, or dizzy — so take your time.

This relaxation method is particularly helpful in producing a
deep physical relaxation and in allowing us to work on areas of
the body that tend to become tense. It is also a useful practice
for relaxing the body if we are having trouble getting to sleep.
Many problems and health difficulties become exaggerated
through lack of sleep. Employing a relaxation technique in bed,
or just before going to bed may be beneficial.

3

Alternate Nostril Breathing

Sitting with their right hands over their faces, the group practise a breathing exercise. Many of them have their eyes closed, concentrating on their breathing. After a few minutes, the tutor chimes a bell and the group drop their hands into their laps and settle into their sitting position.

Breathing exercises can be extremely helpful in promoting physical relaxation, through the process of slowing and deepening the breath. They are also a useful adjunct to meditation as a preliminary practice.

It can be especially useful to employ a breathing exercise in the morning before the demands of your day begin. It may help you become fully awake and refreshed and ready to start the day.

At other times of day, breathing exercises can calm you if you are feeling worked up, or can encourage clarity if you are feeling flat and lacking in energy. Breathing exercises may also have therapeutic benefits, such as helping with pain relief, insomnia, and emotional distress.

Breathing exercise 1 – *Alternate nostril breathing*
(see figures 3-1 and 3-2)

Place the index finger of your right hand on the bridge of your nose, with the finger pointing up towards the top of your head.

Cover and close your right nostril with your thumb and breathe in through the left nostril.

Then cover and close the left nostril with your second finger and uncover and open the right nostril.

Breathe out and then in again.

Uncover and open the left nostril and close the right nostril.

Breathe out and then in again through the left nostril.

Continue in this way, alternately breathing out and then in with each nostril, covering and closing the nostril that is not being used.

Always close the nostril after the in-breath so that you breathe in through one nostril and out through the other.

At first breathe at a normal rate and then gradually breathe more deeply and slowly

A written explanation of this exercise appears complicated, whereas the exercise is in fact quite simple. It may be helpful to ask someone to read the explanation to you while you perform it, and then it will quickly make sense.

This breathing exercise is most useful for clearing the nasal passages, although it can be difficult to perform if you have some congestion. Many people find it helpful to close their eyes whilst practising this exercise and find it extremely calming.

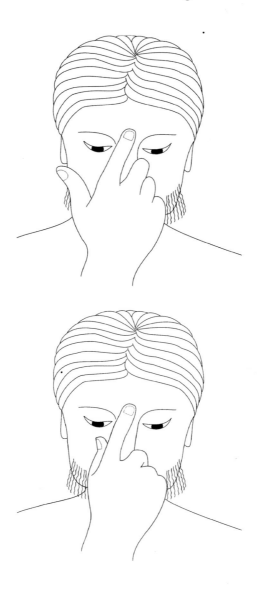

figures 3-1 & 3-2 – *Alternate Nostril Breathing*

4

Listening

The classroom is filled with the lyrical sound of classical music. The lighting is subdued. A group of people sit in a circle. They are not doing anything – just sitting, with their eyes closed, immersed in the flow of the melody.

It is rare that we listen to music just for the experience of *Listening*. We may listen to music while we are walking or engaging in household chores. There may be background music at our place of work. Music can be present in almost all areas of our lives – in shops, on answer phones, in elevators, in taxis. Despite this pervasive presence of music however, it is unusual for us to simply stop and fully engage with the experience of *Listening*. The closest we may come to *Listening* in ordinary life is when we attend a music concert. Even here however, the focus is not entirely on *Listening* because there is also a visual aspect and the interaction of the audience that surrounds us.

In the relaxation technique of *Listening*, that is all we do – we listen. We do not listen and read a book. We do not listen and become fascinated with the contents of the room. We do not listen and analyse the structure of the music. We simply listen.

Relaxation technique 2 – *Listening*

Sit comfortably in a quiet room.
Listen to music.
Do not engage in any other activity whilst listening.
Allow hearing the music to become the totality of your experience.
Continue listening for at least ten minutes.

To help you to focus it may be helpful to subdue the lighting in the room in which you are *Listening*. You may like to use headphones to immerse yourself fully in the experience.
You may wish to close your eyes.

It is important to take care about the choice of music. Classical music is an obvious choice but by no means the only possible option. We could choose any music that we really enjoy, that touches us in some way, and in which we can become fully engrossed.

5

Singing

The group sit in a circle and fill the space in front of them with sound. At times the music of their voices is cacophonous and discordant; a few seconds later it is melodious. Gradually those who were feeling a little timid or self-conscious begin to sing in a more relaxed manner and with gusto. The song swells as individuals experiment with high notes and low notes. The sound is glorious and uplifting. After a little while the group leader stops singing, and slowly those nearest to her notice and also stop singing their note at the end of a breath. The awareness of ceasing ripples through the group until there is silence — a deep and profound silence that contrasts sharply with the loudness of the song. After a few moments of dwelling together in the potent silence, one group member suddenly laughs, saying: "Wow! That was amazing! I've always been told that I can't sing in tune, so it was wonderful to just let myself enjoy making a noise, knowing that it didn't matter what note I produced."

Music and song are a vital aspect of being human and are used to express the complete range of emotions. The use of the voice has a potency, and music animates the lyrics of a song. If we look at the lyrics of most popular songs they are often highly repetitive with the same simple lyric being repeated again and again. That lyric however, combined with a rhythm and a pleasing tune, creates an enjoyable musical experience. Singing words adds a dimension to our experience of those words – it energises and enhances them, adding an emotional component.

The voice is communicative, and through it we convey a broader range of meaning than that which is expressed by the words we use. We use our voices every day to communicate with one another. We communicate with one another through intellectual understanding of spoken words, but we say much more than we may realise through tone, emphasis, facial expression and body language.

Our voices are an energetic aspect of who we are. The sounds we make are 'material' in that they affect our senses, but their 'materiality' is intangible. We cannot touch, taste, smell or see sound. Our voice is the intangible and energetic link between our mind and our body – between our insubstantial being and our substantial being. Practices using the voice help us become keenly aware of the power of this energetic communication.

The practice of *Singing* is an excellent exercise for enabling people to find their voice. Many people are quite nervous and self-conscious about singing and it is something that they generally do not do.

The majority of students in my community education classes would be quite worried about the idea of singing in front of others and reluctant to join in the practice at first.

They may have been told in school that they cannot sing or had friends or family complain about their singing. I find this sad.

Everyone has a voice and everyone can enjoy singing – it is a shame to be denied the pleasure of making noises because of comments by others. To be told that you cannot sing is as much nonsense as to be told you cannot draw or be creative.

Sadly our educational experience often stultifies rather than encourages our creativity. Of course we can sing – if we have vocal cords and breath. Of course we can draw and be creative – if we have a body, the tools for drawing, painting or sculpting and a wish to be creative. No-one can judge our singing or our creativity if it is an expression of who we are and an expression of the joy of having the capacities of a human body.

Singing enables us to let go of our inhibitions and preconceptions about our ability to sing. We open our mouths, and let the sound flow freely with delight. Singing is in itself an invigorating and expansive practice if we allow our voices to be free. It has been wonderful to witness the change in people through this practice. At first a lot of people will barely open their mouths and will find it difficult to produce any sound at all. Once they have practised this a few times however, even the most timid will start to really open their mouths and give voice. In the end this was often one of the favourite practices of most groups.

Relaxation technique 3 – *Singing*

Sing a long extended 'open-vowel A' which sounds like 'Ahhhhhhhhh'.
Sing this sound on every out-breath – open your mouth and let sound arise.
Change the pitch of the sound on each new out-breath.
Let the tone and quality of your voice change continually with each breath.
Experiment with high notes and low notes, harsh notes and sweet notes.
Feel that you are filling the space in front of you with vibrant sound.
Continue for as long as you wish.

This is an extremely simple practice – one simply sings the sound *Ahhhhhhhhh* for the length of the out-breath, changing the note of the sound with each breath. *Ahhhhhhhhh* is the sound that naturally arises when we give voice – it is not created or manipulated, it is simply the basic sound of breath, an open mouth and engaging our voice.

We are not trying to create a tune or something pretty in this practice – we just open our mouths and let song flow forth. It does not matter if you are tone deaf and cannot 'sing in tune' for this practice – you simply enjoy the sound of your voice.

Singing is particularly powerful if practised in a group. Each person's length of breath will be different, so new notes will be starting all the time. Sometimes the effect will be harmonious and sometimes discordant. Lack of harmony does not matter and is part of the experience of the exercise. When the sound is discordant, allow this to be interesting rather than experiencing it as unpleasant.

Occasionally the whole group may coincidentally finish their out-breath at the same moment and there will be an unexpected silence—although often someone will giggle—until an individual begins *Singing* again. Occasionally the whole group may find themselves singing the same note. This is all fine – enter the practice without expectation. There is no right or wrong way to engage with *Singing*.

When practising in a group—especially if some members of the group are nervous about singing—close your eyes. Sit in a circle and feel that you are creating a sphere of sound in front of you – a magnificent, continual sphere of sound. Even a small group of only three or four people can produce a continuous and powerful sound.

When leading a group for this practice, I always sing loudly and strongly to begin with, so that everyone can hear my voice and the more uncertain of the group do not feel that everyone is hearing their voice. Usually people quickly gain in confidence and start to really enjoy being able to let themselves go and make plenty of noise. It is then most powerful if all participants sing quite loudly so that one's individual singing becomes a part of the whole sound and one loses the sense of one's own voice being separate from the whole.

It is important to let the voice flow naturally – to be open and relaxed, and to allow the voice its natural boldness and freedom. It is actually more difficult to sing quietly than to sing loudly, so relax and allow yourself to make a loud sound.

Although *Singing* can be practised alone, it will not be the same experience as practising it in a group. If it is not possible to practise this in a group, you could create a recording of yourself *Singing* for a period of time—or even several recordings—and then sing with your recordings. Singing with a recording will not be the same as experiencing practising this in a group, but will still be enjoyable and help to allow the energy of your voice to flow.

6

Breathing out Tension

The group are spread around the room. Most of them are lying on the floor, with a few sitting in chairs. The room is entirely silent apart from the quiet voice of the tutor leading the breathing practice.

The relaxation technique described in this chapter uses the breath as a focus, and engages our imagination. Ideally this exercise should be practised lying down to achieve the deepest possible benefit, but it can also be practised sitting in a chair if this is preferred.

Breathing exercise 2 – *Breathing out Tension*

Lie in a comfortable position on your back in a room with subdued lighting, ensuring that you are warm.
Bring your attention to your breathing.
Deepen and slow your breathing.
Breathe in through your nose throughout the exercise imagining that the breath flows in to the centre of your chest.
Imagine that you can direct the flow of the out-breath through different parts of the body. and that all tension flows out with the breath.

First of all imagine for several breaths that your breath flows in to the centre of your chest, and then flows out from there through your arms. Imagine that your breath emerges from your finger tips and from the spaces between your fingers, taking away all tension in your arms.

Then for several out-breaths imagine that the out-breath flows from the centre of your chest and down your legs, with all tension in your legs flowing out with the breath.
The breath emerges from the tips of your toes and from the spaces between your toes.

Then direct several out-breaths to flow from your chest down the centre of your body and out of the bottom of your torso between your legs.
Feel that the flow of the out-breath releases all the tension in the organs of the abdomen, and let the stomach muscles become completely relaxed.

Finally imagine that for several out-breaths the flow travels from the centre of the chest upwards and out of the top of your head.
Feel that the breath takes away all tension in the shoulders, neck and face, and all emotional tension and worry with it as it flows out through the top of your head.

Continue with this relaxation imagining the flow of the breath through the body as long as you are comfortable, listening to music if you wish.
Take your time getting up from the relaxation when you finish the session, moving slowly and gently.

Relaxation techniques can lower the blood pressure, so it is important to rouse yourself slowly from a session. Move around a little before sitting or standing, flexing muscles and stretching the body.

In this relaxation, if a colour occurs to you for the out-breath, then you can imagine the out-breath leaving your body as that colour and taking all tension with it. If a colour does not spontaneously arise however, there is no need to create one unless you wish to. If you do wish to imagine the breath as a colour, you could choose a spacious blue, a soothing green, a warming red, a cleansing white, or an enriching gold.

7

Posture

The room is quiet and peaceful. A group of people sit in a circle. Most of them use the ordinary classroom chairs, though some have added the comfort of a cushion. One lady has her feet resting on a yoga block. Another sits on a pile of cushions on the floor using a sitting strap. A young man looks comfortable on a bean bag, and a middle-aged lady is nestled into an inflatable chair. The ages of the group members range from young adult to elderly. They sit motionless for ten minutes without fidgeting, until the bell is chimed to announce the end of the session.

The relaxation techniques described so far have mostly been practised lying down, but from here on a sitting position is likely to be the best posture for the following practices.

If we are going to sit to employ a relaxation technique, breathing exercise, or to meditate, it is important to be as comfortable as possible so that our bodies do not become a hindrance to the practice. We need to be comfortable and physically relaxed in a position that we can hold throughout the practice.

Our posture should enhance our relaxation, breathing exercise or meditation, making it easy for us to fully enter into the practice. We want to sit comfortably so that we do not experience pain in the knees, hips, back, shoulders, or neck.

The primary factors of a good sitting posture are threefold: the body is upright, the body is balanced without straining to hold the position, and the body is unrestricted. The back should be upright and naturally erect, with the shoulders, neck, arms and legs in a position which can be comfortably maintained, and which allows the blood supply to flow freely to all parts of the body. The upright manner of the back needs to allow for the natural curvature of the spine without slumping or being rigidly straight. Tilting the hips forward slightly allows the abdomen to be open and relaxed, and the spine to balance in a naturally vertical position.

The arms, legs and shoulders will be comfortable if the sitting posture is supportive, so that tension does not occur either through trying to hold them in a position, or trying to extend joints beyond their natural flexibility. The chin can be slightly tucked in towards the chest. This helps to lengthen the spine and avoid tension in the neck. Do not let your chin drop right down onto your chest however, as this will make you sleepy and hurt your neck. The arms are best held slightly away from the torso to allow air to circulate at the armpits. To avoid the mouth becoming dry, rest the tongue lightly on the floor of the mouth, or suspend it slightly in the centre of the mouth. Tension can tend to arise if the tongue is clamped onto the palate and this will make the mouth dry.

A common position for practising is sitting cross-legged and there are several styles of this posture. Meditators are often pictured in a cross-legged position known as the *lotus posture*, and this is considered by some to be the perfect meditation posture. In lotus posture the legs are crossed and the feet are brought up to rest on the thighs with the soles of the feet facing uppermost (see figure 7-1). It is an ideal posture for meditation because it requires no cushioning to maintain, provides a secure triangular base to the body, and puts the spine in the correct upright position. Unless you have practised this posture since early childhood however, or are an adept practitioner of yoga, it is unlikely that you will be able to stay in the posture comfortably for more than a few minutes. I would advise against attempting to stay in this posture if it causes you even slight discomfort, as holding it when it is beyond the limit of your joint flexibility can damage the knees and the ankles.

People can sometimes get a little excited about the benefits of full lotus posture and regard it as a spiritual practice in itself. Full lotus posture may be the perfect meditation posture in theory, but in reality the majority of ordinary people cannot achieve it. The important thing is to engage with practice – and practising regularly in any comfortable position is more valuable than achieving a supposedly 'spiritual' sitting position such as the full lotus posture.

There are several less extreme forms of sitting cross-legged that most people *can* achieve. Half lotus posture is more achievable than full lotus. In this posture only one foot is brought up to rest on the thigh.

figure 7-1 – full lotus posture

Other cross-legged positions have one foot resting on the calf of the other leg rather than on the thigh, or both feet on the floor, one in front of the other. Both of these are more easily achieved than full lotus or half lotus.

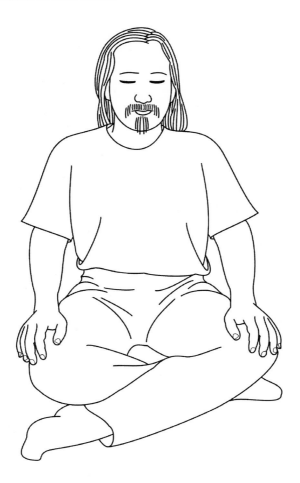

figure 7-2 – cross-legged

When sitting cross-legged it is important to have the hips higher than the knees, so that the knees can hang down and rest on the floor or mat on which you are sitting. Experiment with different heights of cushion under your bottom, until you find the height that rolls the pelvis forward slightly, allowing the knees to be fully supported, and putting the spine in a natural upright and balanced position.

figure 7-3 – cross-legged, side view

It is common to use a large flat cushion on the floor with a round or rectangular cushion on top of it that you sit upon. This arrangement means that your bottom can be at the correct height and your legs are on a warm and soft surface. A thick mat or a sheepskin rug can be used as an alternative to the flat cushion. Some people prefer a rectangular cushion as it can be higher and firmer than a round cushion. Instructions for making a rectangular, round and flat cushion can be found in Appendices A, B and C at the end of the book.

Many people find kneeling to be a comfortable position for meditation, and kneeling is a good posture for keeping the spine in an upright position (figure 7-4). You can use your round or rectangular cushion between your legs to raise the hips well above the knees, or you can buy a special kneeling stool. There are two main types of kneeling stool in common use. The first is like a small, sloping table which is placed over the legs and sat upon. The second type looks like a toadstool, where you place your legs either side of the 'stalk' and sit on the crown of the toadstool. The table-like stools can be quite convenient as they often fold flat for storage and transportation. Kneeling chairs are also comfortable because they are effective in placing the spine in a naturally upright ergonomic position.

When kneeling, it is especially important to ensure that blood flow to the legs is not restricted, and that the knee joints are not over-stretched or have too much pressure put upon them.

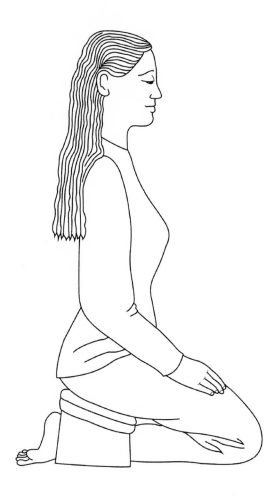

figure 7-4 – kneeling

For many people—particularly if you are starting to practise these relaxation and meditation techniques later in life—sitting in a chair is the best choice. There is no reason at all why you should not use a chair for relaxation techniques, breathing exercises and meditation practice. Sometimes people can be purist about meditation and insist that one should sit in a 'spiritual' position. However if a 'spiritual' position means physical torment throughout your practice session, then adopting such a position is pointless. It is far more important for the body to be comfortable so that you can stay relaxed and focused in your practice.

Care should be taken in choosing a chair for sitting practice. It must support the spine and not cause your back to slump. Slumping will create problems in your back and also tend to make you dull and sleepy. If the chair has arms they must not be so high that they lift the shoulders and prevent your arms from hanging in a natural position, as this will create tension in the shoulders, back and neck. Finally the seat of the chair must be at the correct height for your stature. Your legs, with feet resting on the floor, should bend at the knee with a 90° angle. If the chair is too high for you, place something under your feet. This will ensure that your thighs can remain horizontal and that there is not undue pressure behind the knees. If the chair is too low for you, add cushions to the seat.

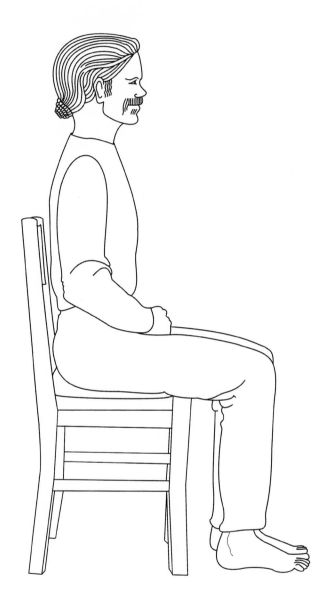

figure 7-5 – sitting in a chair

My personal preferred position for sitting is on a high firm cushion on a sheepskin rug, using a sitting strap. This strap is a simple and clever Tibetan device to help maintain a comfortable sitting posture. It goes around the knees and back and provides support so that the body can relax into the sitting position. You can find instructions for making a sitting strap in Appendix D.

figure 7-6 – using a sitting strap

There is nothing wrong—in theory—with practising standing up or lying down, but there are disadvantages to each posture. If we attempt to practise standing up, our blood pressure may drop owing to the quietening effect of our breathing exercise, relaxation or meditation, which could cause us to experience dizziness or become light-headed. For most of us, standing will not be a practical posture for the methods I describe, and will not be a position that is comfortable to maintain for any length of time.

Lying down is fine in terms of it being a comfortable position that is supportive and will not create any tension in the body. It is ideal for relaxation but it is not conducive to remaining alert. Hence sitting in some form is usually the best posture for the exercises that follow.

8

Rhythm Breathing

The group, sitting in front of the group leader, try to follow the movements she is making with her hand. Several people catch on immediately and are able to follow, but others are finding it difficult. The tension is released when one lady who is struggling suddenly bursts out laughing. "I think the problem is that I am sitting opposite you, so I am having to try to mirror what you are doing. Can I come and sit by you instead?" The leader is happy for her to do this, and a couple of other people also move their chairs. This helps considerably, and soon the whole group is performing the movements like a hand ballet and focusing on their breathing, as the leader slowly, quietly and rhythmically intones: "Breathe-in, two, three, four; hold, two, three, four; breathe-out, two, three, four."

Having established a comfortable sitting posture, let us now look at another breathing exercise. This exercise, and the two relaxation techniques that follow in the next two chapters— *Candle Flame* and *Om, A'a & Hung*—mark a transition between relaxation practice and meditation practice.

These practices will function as relaxation methods at this stage. Once some experience of meditation has been gained and its principle and function understood, these methods may be revisited and used as meditation.

Breathing exercise 3 – *Rhythm breathing*

Breathe in to the count of four.
Hold the breath to the count of four.
Breathe out to the count of four.
Continue this pattern in an even rhythm.

The count must be slow and even and there is a hand movement that is used to accompany the exercise to help maintain an even rhythm and speed (see figures 8-1 – 8-5.)

Place the right hand with the palm uppermost on the right knee.
Breathing in, count 1 as the hand makes a large, graceful arc across and above your knees to arrive palm downwards on your left knee.
Continuing to breathe in, reverse this movement for the count of 2, so that the hand makes another graceful arc across and above the knees until it comes to rest once more on the right knee with the palm uppermost.
Continuing to breathe in for the count of 3, the hand rises up in another graceful arc to touch a point slightly behind the left shoulder.
Continuing to breathe in, the hand is then returned to the right knee palm uppermost, and the fingers are snapped on the count of 4 to mark the end of the cycle of breathing in.

This hand movement is then repeated for the 4 counts of the breath being held, and again for the 4 counts of the out-breath.

Breathing in should take the whole length of the count of four. Then the breath is held for four. Breathing out should also take the whole length of the count of four.

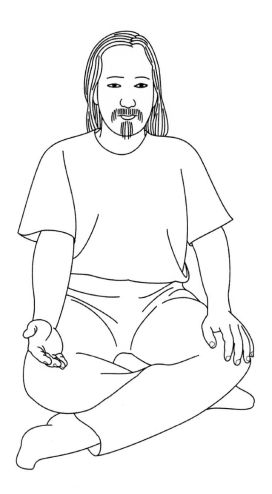

figure 8-1 – rhythm breathing starting position

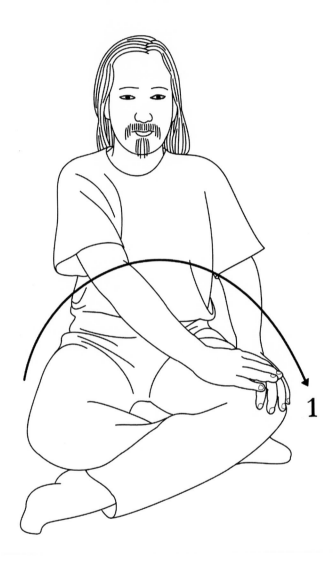

figure 8-2 – rhythm breathing, count 1

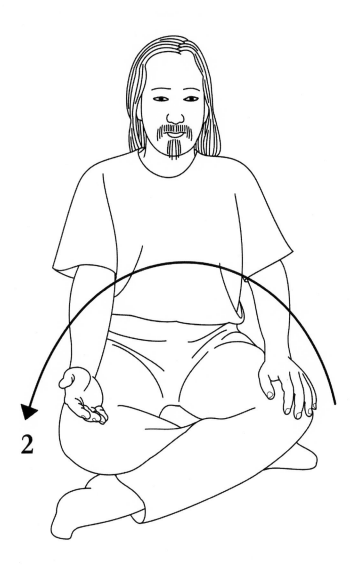

figure 8-3 – rhythm breathing, count 2

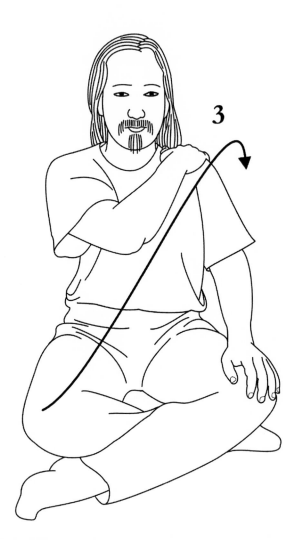

figure 8-4 – rhythm breathing, count 3

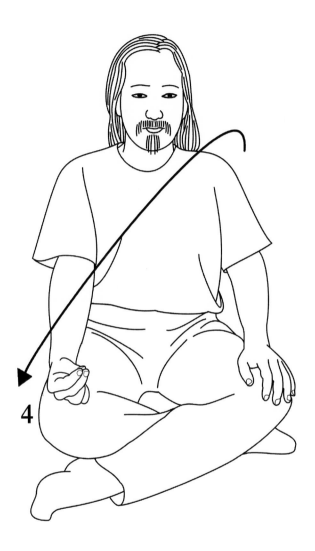

4

figure 8-5 – rhythm breathing, count 4

The part of the cycle where the breath is held is simply a suspension of breathing. The in-breath ceases and there is a pause before the out-breath begins. The breath is not locked or the throat closed to hold the breath in – breathing-in simply stops and breathing is suspended for the count of four, until breathing out commences. Breathe in for the count of four, cease breathing and suspend the breath for the count of four, breathe out for the count of four.

Continue with the 4:4:4 count until it is easy and relaxed. When this has been achieved, increase the length of the *held* breath only to a count of 6, so that the pattern becomes 4:6:4 – breathe in for four, hold for six, breathe out for four. The hand movement for the held breath is adjusted to accommodate the longer count. For a count of 6 (4 + 2), the movement of the hand to the point just behind the left shoulder is repeated once more – so that the cycle is: hand over to left knee; hand back to right knee; hand to shoulder; hand back to knee; hand to shoulder; hand back to knee and snap fingers.

This breathing exercise is a progressive increase of lengthening the breath and the hold. The length of breath and hold should not be increased until it feels that the current length is easy to practise. Care should be taken not to simply increase the speed of the count in order to increase the number of the count. The purpose is to gradually lengthen the breath and the suspension of breath. Moving into the longer breath and/or hold should not cause difficulties in breathing so that it is a struggle to maintain, or create agitation in the mind.

When the 4:6:4 counted breathing becomes easy and relaxed, increase the count for the hold to 8. For a count of 8 (4 + 4) the hand movement is adjusted so that the cycle of the hand movement for a count of 4 is repeated. However the fingers are only snapped on the last count of the movement to mark the count of eight.

The pattern of progression of the practice of in-breath, hold and out-breath is as follows:
4:4:4 / 4:6:4 / 4:8:4 / 6:6:6 / 6:8:6 / 6:10:6 / 8:8:8.

When you have moved into breathing in and breathing out for a count of six, once again the breathing in and breathing out should encompass the entire length of the count.

Do not be in a hurry to progress through the sequence. Pushing yourself too hard or too quickly can work against the benefits of *Rhythm Breathing*.

Breathing exercises create spaciousness and calmness in the mind, just as fast breathing can create nervous agitation. If you try to progress in this practice beyond your capability or too fast you may find that your mind becomes unsettled.

9

Candle Flame

The faces of the meditation group adopt a rosy hue in the subdued candlelight. They sit in a circle around a large candle burning brightly. All are quiet as they gaze into the warm light of the candle flame, in the dark room only lit by its glow. Their eyes follow the flame as it gently moves and occasionally flickers.

Relaxation technique 4 – *Candle Flame*

Sit in a comfortable posture in front of a lit candle.
Gaze at the candle flame.
Allow the experience of the candle flame to become expansive.
As you gaze at the flame, experience its colour.
As you gaze at the flame, experience its warmth.
As you gaze at the flame, experience its movement.
As you gaze at the flame, experience the scent and taste of the hot wax.
Continue in this way for as long as is comfortable, and for as long as you feel present and engaged by the experience of the candle flame.

Choose a large candle with a good wick that will produce a strong flame. If possible, place the candle where it will experience a slight draft so that the flame moves gently and is not completely stationary. Darken the room and place the candle in front of you at a height which is comfortable for resting your eyes on the flame.

Gaze with a relaxed focus that includes all your senses and not just your sight, so that all physical sensation arising through the senses is experienced within the context of the candle flame. Gaze without expectation of what you might see or experience.

Care must always be taken with naked flames. Be sure that you are safe and that the candle is burning on a stable surface in a heat-resistant container. Apart from this particular relaxation technique, I generally advise against having candles in line of sight in the room in which you practise relaxation or meditation. They can become a distraction.

I would also not recommend the use of incense. The scent of incense is pleasant, but the smoke is as harmful as any smoke when taken into the lungs. If you wish the room in which you practise relaxation or meditation to smell of incense, I would suggest burning it in there prior to your practice session, so that you have the benefit of the scent without the smoke. Incense smoke is particularly inadvisable if you are engaging in breathing exercises or practices that involve singing, as the deeper breathing created through these exercises will mean the smoke is taken deeply into your lungs. This is harmful and will tend to make you cough.

10

Om, A'a & Hung – Relaxation

The group sing syllables over and over in a rhythmic fashion.
The sound is rich and sonorous, seeming to vibrate deeply
within each of the practitioners.

The next relaxation technique uses the voice, employing three
syllables that are used in many Buddhist practices. The syllables
are used as a means of inspiring awareness of certain points on
the body. In this practice, the object of the exercise is to create
an energetic awareness of the forehead, throat and central chest
area through the resonance of the syllables at these places on the
body. The Tibetan syllable which is written as *A'a* is simply
sounded as an *'A'* sound.

Relaxation technique 5 – *Singing Om, A'a & Hung*

Sing the syllables in turn, using the same note and pitch.
Sing each syllable for the length of an out-breath.
Sing the syllables over and over in turn.
Feel the vibration of Om at the forehead.
Feel the vibration of A'a at the throat.
Feel the vibration of Hung at the centre of the chest.

This practice can be practised alone as effectively as in a group. If practising in a group, decide upon a leader who chooses the note to be sung and the length of time it is held. If your breath is longer than that of the song leader, stop singing the syllable when the leader stops. If your breath is shorter, pause until the song leader begins the next syllable.

figure 10-1 – Om, A'a, Hung
calligraphy by Ngakpa Chögyam

11

Fruit of Relaxation

"I feel it will help me to relax."
"My job is quite stressful. Meditation will help me."
"I want to understand who I am."
"It looks like a cool thing to do."
"Some of my friends meditate and they seem to be happier and calmer than me."

Relaxation techniques and breathing exercises enable us to be calmer human beings. Through learning to quieten the breath and relax the body, we can approach the circumstances of our lives in a calmer and more relaxed manner. Discovering relaxation offers the opportunity to begin to practise meditation, because we will find that our minds are ready to become more open and spacious. Relief from stress and tension enables us to take our practice to the next stage.

We may have observed than when we are in a state of raised anxiety our breathing becomes faster and more shallow. The slower and deeper breathing promoted through the relaxation techniques and breathing exercises we have learned, will reduce our anxiety and enable us to be more relaxed.

Once we are familiar with these practices we can use them in our everyday life to help us to be calmer in all circumstances. If you are having a stressful day at work, practice breathing out tension for a few moments when you have the opportunity. If your children are challenging your capacity to remain calm and good natured, engage them in *Singing* – they will enjoy the opportunity to make noise and also become calmer and more settled themselves. If your life circumstances are painful or worrying, give yourself time to practise a relaxation technique – it will make the situation easier to deal with.

Once we have become used to calming ourselves through relaxation techniques and breathing exercises, we are ready to approach meditation practice.

One of the first questions that arises when introducing people to meditation, is 'why meditate?' What is the purpose of meditation and why would anyone wish to do it? How can sitting still with my eyes closed for a period of time be of benefit to me? Why would I wish to move on from relaxation to meditation?

Meditation offers benefits at every level – physical, emotional, intellectual and spiritual. Sitting quietly, visualising, singing or focusing on the breath, calms and relaxes the body. It calms and relaxes the mind. It calms and relaxes the energy of who we are. Meditation enables us to unravel unhelpful emotional fixations. Our intellect can become clearer and more focused through allowing the chatter of our minds to subside. We can discover the nature of who we are at a deep and profound level through meditative practice.

Starting to meditate can be a little like stepping off the roller coaster of our lives for a while to let it rattle by. It can also enable us to continue to ride the roller coaster but with greater awareness and enjoyment.

Many people believe that the practice of meditation is esoteric or exotic – something connected to Eastern culture. They are unsure as to whether it is a relevant or accessible activity for 'ordinary' everyday folk. The word 'meditation' conjures up for them images of people surrounded by candles, sitting in difficult yogic postures, holding their hands in 'mystic' positions with serene expressions on their faces. This idea has most probably arisen from the media view of meditation portrayed in films and television programmes. Whenever anyone is shown engaging in meditation in such genres they will generally be surrounded by many candles, or be seated in front of a candle. They are also often sitting cross-legged with their knees raised up too high and unsupported, and with their arms and hands in tense, uncomfortable positions.

Meditation however, is in fact a simple method of exercising awareness, that can hone our capacity to concentrate, develop direct perception, and ultimately enable us to discover total relaxation of mind and body. Meditation can be regarded as a useful exercise for each and every one of us. It is as important to our psychological health as physical exercise is to our physical well-being.

Meditation can be a deep spiritual experience, or it can be practised simply as a beneficial exercise – in the way that we may practise keep fit, yoga or pilates.

'Meditation' is a generic term that may be used in the same way as we use the word 'music'. 'Music' can encompass a classical sonata, a traditional folk song, jazz, heavy metal, rock and roll, blues, Gregorian chant – the list could be almost endless. Similarly the term 'meditation' may be used to cover a range of practices – guided meditation, visualisation, chanting, spiritual analysis and concentration For a practice to be meditation, it must have a clear principle and function. It must direct the experience of the meditator towards opening and clarifying the mind through the application of effort and attention.

To achieve relaxation of mind—as well as relaxation of body— we need to examine and understand our mind. We need to *know* our mind through direct experience, rather than through an endless spate of discursive thought. We can start to learn to relax into meditation.

12

Letting Go

"Let go of the busy-ness of your day and the concerns of your life. Settle into your meditation posture and bring your attention to your breathing." The group, sitting in a half circle around the tutor, take a few moments to adjust their position. Gradually they all stop fidgeting and sit silently without moving. An atmosphere of tranquil alertness fills the room. It feels like a space taken out of time — as though life has become hushed and suspended for a while.

Having prepared ourselves to begin to meditate through relaxation and breathing exercises, we are ready to learn meditation methods. It will now become particularly important to ensure that we are comfortable in our sitting position, so perhaps take a few minutes to review the section on sitting postures in chapter 7. Meditation is sometimes called *sitting*, and it is good to try to remain still for the whole period of our meditation session. If it is really necessary to move—to stretch an uncomfortable limb or deal with an itch—then that is fine, but if we find that we are continually fidgeting it will be difficult to fully engage with the meditation method.

Ideally we should rise from our session with the body feeling relaxed and invigorated through the calmness of mind and body we have discovered through our meditation. Relaxation of the body will facilitate relaxation of the mind.

If we are experiencing discomfort it can become distracting, so that the focus of our meditation will tend to be pulled to the sensation of discomfort rather than the intended focus of the practice. If your practice session becomes *meditation on the pain in my knees*, it will be an unhelpful distraction.

Special mention must be made of the eyes in meditation. Many people begin with their eyes closed for meditation practice – but this is not necessarily the best choice. Closing the eyes is excellent for avoiding distractions of sight, but can tend to make the mind dull and encourage a state of introversion. In meditation we wish to avoid distraction, but not to the point of cutting ourselves off from our environment and withdrawing into an inner world. We wish to remain alert, focused and present with the meditation practice. We should be fully aware of where we are, not withdrawn into an other-worldly state.

To avoid the tendency for introversion, meditate with the eyes slightly open and gazing downwards. This is a preferable posture to having the eyes closed. Having the eyes slightly open allows a little light to enter them so that the mind is less likely to become dull and sleepy, but without the distractions of the environment impinging.

The primary purpose of the first meditation method is to get to know our mind through direct experience. In order to do this we let go of our involvement with our thought processes, so that we can discover who we are when we are no longer thinking.

It is not that thought is a problem—it is an essential aspect of being human—it is just that we use thought constantly to engage with and interpret our existence. We experience thought as a continual, endless stream, so that we have no knowledge of *mind without thought*.

Meditation method 1 – *Letting Go*

Stage I – *using counting the breath as a focus*

Bring your attention to your breathing. Do not attempt to change the quality or rhythm of your breathing – simply use the breath as a focus.
Begin to count the out-breaths.
Count each out-breath from one up to twenty-one, and then count each out-breath from twenty-one back down to one.
This is one cycle.
Throughout this practice, if thought arises, let it go. Do not engage with the content of the thought, but return to counting the out-breaths.
Repeat the cycle as many times as you wish.

This is where we begin with our meditation practice. Practise it now for one round of counting up to twenty-one out-breaths and then back down to one. Do this before reading the next paragraph so that you have an experience of this stage of the practice before hearing about the next stage, and before learning what may occur.

The purpose of this stage of the practice is to give ourselves something to focus upon so that we are less distracted by thought and are less inclined to become involved in the content of our thoughts.

There are commonly three types of loss of awareness that are experienced during this practice:

1. the count is lost completely as the mind wanders off on a thought-story;

2. the count is retained but there is insufficient awareness to note the arrival at the count of twenty-one, so that a higher number is reached before one suddenly becomes aware of the count again;

3. the count is confused because we no longer know whether we are counting up from one to twenty-one or back down from twenty-one to one.

Whenever we realise that awareness has been lost through losing track of the count, we simply return to one and begin to count again. We do not become cross or frustrated at losing track of what number we are on – in fact we celebrate the moment of realising that the count has been lost because this is a moment of *re-emerging awareness*. This is the moment when we are aware once again and able to return to the practice. Every time we realise that we have lost the count, we have in fact found it again – so this is a reason to feel happy.

If we know the count—the number we are on, where the count is going, which part of the count cycle we are in—then this is a sign of being *aware in the present moment*.

Gradually our capacity to stay with counting the out-breaths increases and we are able to remain with it for several rounds with ease – thoughts may arise, but they no longer distract us sufficiently that we lose our place in the count.

Once we are able to stay with this practice, we can then move on to the second stage of *Letting Go*.

Staying with counting the breath indefinitely however, is fine as a meditation practice and will bring benefits, so there is no need to feel any pressure or obligation to move on to the second stage of the practice quickly. You may find that a point naturally arises where you no longer wish to count the breath—where you feel sufficiently focused and present to spontaneously let go of the count—and so at that time move on to the second stage.

Stage II – *using the mere awareness of the breath as a focus*

Bring your attention to your breathing. Do not attempt to change the quality or rhythm of your breathing – simply use the breath as a focus. As you breathe out, let go of any thought arising in the mind and rest in the empty space of mind without thought.
Continue in this way, letting go of whatever thoughts arise in the mind as you breathe out.

Here the focus of counting the out-breaths is dropped, and the merest awareness of the out-breath remains. Counting the out-breaths has served as an anchor to hold the awareness of the mind, and as a means to take our attention away from the fascination of thought.

63

Once the compulsion to think all the time has reduced and we start to feel more comfortable about letting go of thought, then we can move on from the method of counting and hone our concentration with a more subtle focus.

Continue with Stage II until you are beginning to experience periods of quietness and emptiness of mind – noticeable periods of *mind without thought*. These periods may only be brief flashes of empty mind to begin with, which are quickly dissolved through noticing them. It can become rather amusing at this stage of our practice—though perhaps frustrating—to watch ourselves destroying a moment of mind without thought: *'Heh, I'm not thinking! Oh drat... that was a thought!'* Eventually however we will discover longer periods of stillness. As soon as such periods are happening regularly, we can move on to the formless practice of *Letting Go* if wished – however once again it must be stressed that there is no problem with staying at the stage of using the focus of the breath indefinitely if preferred.

Stage III – *formless practice*

Sit quietly allowing thought to naturally dissolve, without becoming involved in its content or movement.
Continually let go of thought.
Rest in the space of empty, quiet mind, as thought dissolves.
Remain in that space as long as possible.
If thought arises, simply let it go and return to mind without thought.

These three stages of the practice of *Letting Go* become increasingly formless and more subtle. In sequence—as described above—they also become increasingly more demanding in terms of the capacity that is required for maintaining concentration and awareness in the moment. In reality these practices are not used in such a linear manner and the meditator will move between them as seems appropriate for their state of mind in any particular meditation session.

In this practice it is a relaxed and spacious concentration that is required – not tightness and attempting to have strong control. This could be compared to the tension required when knitting a garment. If the tension is too loose, the knitted fabric becomes too floppy and the stitches are holey. If the tension is too tight, the knitted fabric becomes too rigid and the stitches too dense.

Once you are familiar with all three stages of *Letting Go*, you can move between them as appropriate. You could begin your meditation session by starting with Stage III—simply and spontaneously letting go of thought—and see what happens. If you find that the mind is excitable and it is difficult to let go, you can then switch to Stage I or II of *Letting Go* that incorporate focus on the breath. You could use any combination of the three methods in any order that seems helpful and appropriate for your meditation session. Even an experienced meditator may begin a session with a round or two of counting the breath, as a useful means of gauging their level of awareness and capacity to focus.

The fruit of the practice of *Letting Go* is the ability to dwell, for extended periods of time, in a state of emptiness, *mind without thought* – a state of alert presence where thought is no longer arising. This is a state of relaxed attention; a state of tranquil concentration. It is not cut off from the world – it is simply empty. Once we arrive in this space we may discover it is surprisingly easy to remain there. Learning to rest comfortably in this space of *mind without thought* opens many possibilities for further practice and for the development of awareness.

Letting Go is a ground or fundamental practice. As well as revealing the nature of the mind, when practised regularly *Letting Go* will increase our ability to focus and concentrate. These are qualities that are essential if we wish to explore other types of meditation. To engage in practices of visualisation—for example—it is necessary to be able to focus clearly and concentrate on the form of the visualisation. This will not be possible if our mind is continually distracted by errant thought patterns or is sleepy and dull.

Regular practise of *Letting Go* will change our relationship with thought, and it is this change and discovering *mind without thought,* that eventually leads to true relaxation of mind and body.

13

Refreshing Stretch

The group have spread themselves out around the room. Two people remain seated while the rest of the group are standing. Following the instructions of the tutor they perform an exercise which involves stretching, bending and deep breathing. Long, audible exhalations accompany the movement. The two people sitting in chairs join in with the second half of the exercise. After three repetitions everyone sits down and settles quietly into meditation practice.

If you are new to meditation you may find it quite difficult to sit still and remain comfortable and focused for any length of time. Interspersed among the descriptions of the meditation methods that follow are a number of exercises that can help you stay alert, focused and comfortable while engaging in meditation practice.

Breathing exercise 4 – *refreshing stretch (standing)*
(see figures 13-1 – 13-6)
Stand with your feet a shoulder width apart and your arms hanging down by your sides. Keeping the arms straight, breathe in and raise your arms in front of you and upwards until they are vertically above you. Breathe out as you point your fingers to the sky and feel that you are stretching the whole length of your body.

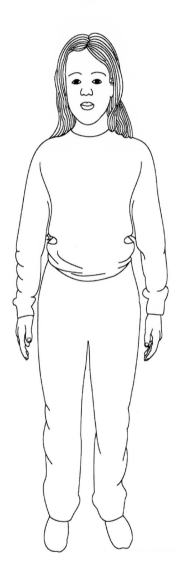

figure 13-1 – *Refreshing Stretch* starting position

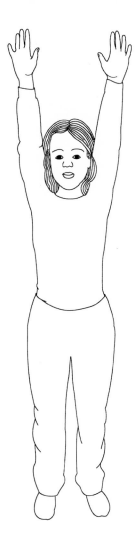

figure 13-2 – *Refreshing Stretch:* stretching up

Breathe in.

As you breathe out, bend at the hips to a point where your body forms a right angle; your back is flat with the arms either side of the ears and your fingers stretched in front of you. Your legs are straight.

figure 13-3 – *Refreshing Stretch:* bend at hip

Holding the position, breathe in.

Breathing out, continue the bend downwards until your fingers touch the floor, and the body is folded in half at the hips. Bring your body in as close to the thighs as possible and your head as low to the floor, whilst keeping the legs straight.

Breathe in.

As you breathe out, relax the body down a little lower, touching the floor with your fingers—even putting the palms of your hands on the floor if you are able—whilst keeping the legs straight.

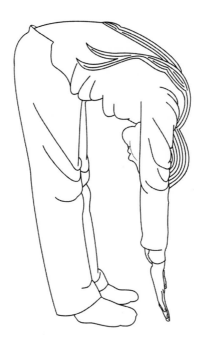

figure 13-4 – *Refreshing Stretch:* full bend

Breathe in.

Breathing out, slowly raise the body up from the bend by gradually unfolding until you are standing upright once more, and then raise your arms above your head.

Breathe in.

As you breathe out stretch upwards. You can go up onto tiptoes to increase the stretch if you wish and have sufficient balance.

figure 13-5 – *Refreshing Stretch:* stretch up

Breathe in.

As you breathe out, and keeping your arms straight, bring them down to your sides in a graceful arc so that you are once more standing in the starting posture.

Repeat the exercise twice more – or as many times as you wish.

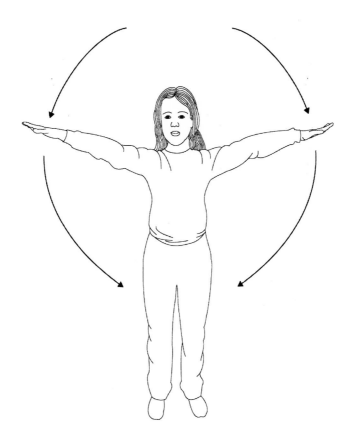

figure 13-6 – *Refreshing Stretch:* arms down to sides

This exercise refreshes and revitalises the body, and does not take a long time to perform. It can be used during a meditation session to energise oneself and cut through sleepiness or distraction. The exercise promotes deep breathing, so take care that you do not become light-headed. Rise back up to the standing position slowly. It is important that the back is kept straight during the downward bend.

If you find this exercise too demanding, are elderly or disabled, it can be practised in a simpler form sitting on a chair. The simpler form can also be useful during a meditation session as you can perform the *Refreshing Stretch* without disturbing your sitting position.

Breathing exercise 4 – *refreshing stretch (sitting)*

(figures 13-7 – 13-9)

Sit on a chair with your arms hanging by your sides.

Breathe in.
As you breathe out raise your arms in front of you and upwards until they are above your head.

Breathe in.
As you breathe out, stretch upwards pointing your fingers towards the sky and feeling the whole of the upper body stretching.

Breathe in.
As you breathe out, and keeping your arms straight, bring your arms down to your sides in a graceful arc so that you are once more sitting in the starting posture.

Repeat the exercise twice more – or as many times as you wish.

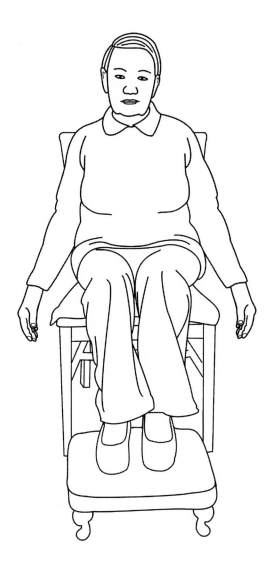

figure 13-7 – *Refreshing Stretch:* starting position, sitting

figure 13-8 – *Refreshing Stretch:* stretch up, sitting

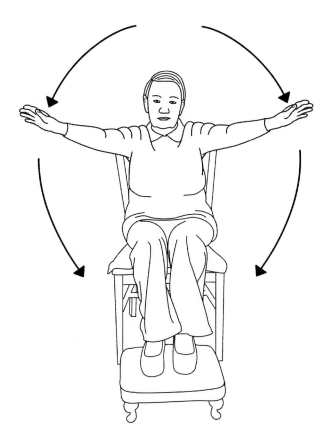

figure 13-9 – *Refreshing Stretch:* arms down, sitting

This version of the exercise is still effective in producing a deep, refreshing breath, but is less likely to make you light-headed. It will also be less demanding for people with back problems, other health conditions, or for the elderly.

14

Daily Practice

"Bring your attention to your breathing. As you breathe out, let go of whatever arises in the mind... Let go of thought... Focus on the out-breath and breathe away the content of mind, letting it go... If you find it is difficult to concentrate, count the out-breaths from one up to twenty-one, and then from twenty-one back down to one, continuing to let go of thought on the out-breath." Having opened the meditation session with this introduction, the tutor says nothing more, and the group sit quietly for ten minutes.

Letting Go is the ground of meditation practice and the base from which all other methods can arise. It is ideal to establish *Letting Go* as a primary daily practice over a considerable period of time. It is not possible to fully engage with other methods, such as visualisation and analysis, without sufficient capacity to concentrate and focus. Engaging with the practice of *Letting Go* will bring many small benefits through the space it develops in the mind, and ultimately will enable the practitioner—with guidance—to gain direct understanding of the mind.

It is essential to establish a daily meditation practice. The power of meditation can be likened to the power of the Colorado River which created the Grand Canyon. The river is not particularly forceful or ferocious, but it has nevertheless created one of the deepest and most spectacular gorges on our planet. The river has slowly, but persistently eroded the landscape through which it flows.

Similarly, if we slowly and persistently apply ourselves to *Letting Go*, it will gradually make a big difference in our lives. It will gradually erode neuroses and patterning. We will find that it will change our outlook and the way in which we respond to the circumstances of our lives. Simple daily practice will gradually enable us to become less stressed, less emotionally churned up by the things that happen to us, and more relaxed about who we are. We can also become less focused on ourselves and more aware of the needs of others. All this is possible with continued application to practice.

It is important to say something here about change. Engaging in meditation will cause us to change. This is inevitable. Any new venture upon which we embark will change us – through contact with new people, new ideas and new experiences. Some people are afraid of change. They want to be happier – but without changing their lives. They want to think deeply and be more spiritual – but not address their attitudes and habit patterns. They want to be kinder, nicer people – but without letting go of their prejudices and preconceptions.

If you begin to engage with meditation practice regularly you will change as a person, because aspects of yourself will be revealed and hidden views will be laid bare. It is important to recognise this and take this into account before beginning meditation practice.

Initially our daily meditation session should be short so that it is easily achievable. It is important to set ourselves a realistic goal that we can succeed in fulfilling. I suggest that people start with a practice of ten minutes meditation every day. Ten minutes is not a great length of time and even the busiest of people can find ten minutes in their day to stop their activities and meditate.

Sometimes beginners are so enthused by learning about meditation and understanding its benefits, that they feel that ten minutes a day must be much too short a length of time to have any benefit. They finish a course, or leave a retreat, full of energy and enthusiasm, determined to practise meditation for an hour a day.

Unfortunately it can be rather difficult to maintain such an ambitious session length on a daily basis, once they are back home in their familiar environment, without the support of other practitioners, and with all the distractions and demands on their time that their lives involve. They may succeed in practising for an hour a day for a few days. They may even manage an hour a day several times a week for a few weeks, but gradually the demands of their lives wear away their good intentions, and their connection with the inspiration for their enthusiasm weakens.

They become discouraged with themselves because they are not achieving the hour of meditation every day that they set out to achieve. Sadly many people give up meditation at this point.

Hence I ask people to set themselves up for success. I ask them to set realistic and achievable goals. Decide to practise for *ten minutes a day* – even if this sounds like a ridiculously short period of time. The point is that it *is* a short period of time – and therefore highly achievable.

Everyone can find ten minutes in their day to stop what they are doing and engage with meditation practice. Some meditation practices require a high degree of concentration and this can be challenging. However it should still be possible to maintain a daily practice of ten minutes even when it is a struggle, because ten minutes is not a long period of time. We can bear the struggle if it is only for a short time.

If we decide to practise for an hour but find that we are struggling even after five minutes, it is hard to stick with our resolve and sit it out for another fifty-five minutes. Our meditation may become an hour of misery – battling with distraction or sleepiness, enduring the pain in our knees or back, or the ache in our neck and shoulders... There is the danger then that our meditation session will become one of watching the clock and wishing that the time would pass more quickly; or of fidgeting continually so that it is impossible to settle into our meditation; or of dozing off uncomfortably for periods of time.

In a ten minute session however, it is unlikely that we will encounter such problems. If we are experiencing physical discomfort, sleepiness or distraction, it is reasonable to work with it for the completion of a ten minute session. Knowing that our meditation is only a short period will enable us to relax if we are struggling, rather than tensing and becoming frustrated during the session.

Setting ourselves a realistic and achievable goal for the length of our meditation session gives us a lot of energy to fulfil this commitment, and a great sense of satisfaction every time we do complete a ten minute session.

At the end of ten minutes there is always the opportunity to sit for a further five minutes if our practice is going well, knowing that we have already fulfilled the goal we set ourselves. If we find that we have actually sat and meditated for fifteen or twenty minutes sometimes – then that is something to feel satisfied about: the goal has been achieved and more.

Continue to set yourself up for success in this way, and do not be in too much of a hurry to increase the length of your meditation sessions. If you find that you are regularly sitting for fifteen minutes or more every day, then at that time you can decide to change your daily commitment to practise meditation for fifteen minutes a day. Do not do this however, before you are sure that you are ready, and that the circumstances of your life will continue to allow you to meet your goal.

It will always be better to do more than you have set out to achieve every day, than to manage it some days and not others. There is also always the option of having a second or third short session of meditation during your day as a way of increasing your practice.

Only increase your personal promise to yourself about the length of your meditation session when you are really sure that you will continue to be able to fulfil it – and enjoy fulfilling it.

It is much more valuable to practise for a short period of time every day, than it is to practise for a longer period a few times a week, or to have one long session a week. Here we could return to the Colorado River analogy – it is the continual action of the water on the landscape that created the Grand Canyon.

The effect of a daily short meditation practice is more potent than irregular longer practice. A short daily practice establishes a good pattern of discipline and effort right from the beginning, and it minimises the possibility of our meditation practice becoming a chore. Our daily meditation becomes part of the ground of who we are. We brush our teeth, we wash up the dishes, we feed the cat… we meditate. We no longer have to decide whether we are going to meditate today because that decision has already been made. Eventually meditation becomes part of our routine like combing our hair. We do not have to think about it, plan for it, or work out how we are going to find time for it – it is simply part of our daily life. Once our daily meditation has become part of who we are, we can start to make real progress.

Eventually in order to gain real insight through meditation and to deepen their experience, many people find that they want to meditate for longer periods of time. Whether you go on to long sessions of meditation will depend on your motivation for practice and the benefits you discover.

This can be considered as a long term aim by the beginner. We recognise the aim and then forget about it for the time being. Even if your daily session only ever remains at around twenty minutes a day, this is certainly sufficient to experience the benefits of meditation.

Traditionally early in the morning is said to be a good time of day to practise and for many this can also be convenient. It may be helpful to start the day with practice before all the demands and distractions of our lives have begun. Personally I also quite like to meditate late at night and am often more awake and focused at this time of day than I am first thing in the morning. There is no incorrect time of day to practise – and *actually* getting down to practice is much more important than the time of day at which you practise.

As to where we practise, this will depend on the space and opportunities available to us. Few of us are lucky enough to be able to dedicate a room in our home to meditation practice, but perhaps we can establish a corner of our bedroom, living room or study as a place for meditation.

It is good to have our meditation cushion, stool or chair set up ready for us, so that it is easy to settle into a daily routine. It can be pleasant to meditate outside if the weather is fine. In fact in theory it is possible to meditate anywhere and everywhere, but beginners will find that a quiet place, free of distracting decoration and noises will be helpful.

15

Head Jerks

Everyone in the chaotic classroom is meditating.
No-one moves. No-one makes a sound.
Suddenly an individual moves their head upwards sharply,
and then repeats the movement twice more.
No-one takes any notice and the individual then returns once
more to sitting completely still.

Once we have established a daily practice of *Letting Go* we will
often find that there are two main obstacles to discovering
awareness in the present moment – namely sleepiness and
distraction. Sleepiness is when the mind is dull and lacks
sharpness and focus – or we may actually find ourselves nodding
off to sleep. Distraction is when we keep getting caught up in
the thoughts that arise in our mind, so that we lose awareness of
the present moment.

The next technique is a simple physical aid to help with this.

Meditation aid 1 – *Head Jerks*

If you are feeling distracted—the mind is too busy and full of thought, and you are not able to let it dissolve—practise this simple exercise:

Tip your head back slightly.
Then bring the head forwards sharply, dropping your chin on to your chest.
The movement must be fairly quick and vigorous, but take care not to jar the neck.
Practise this movement three times and then return to your meditation.

If you are feeling dull or sleepy—the mind is unfocused and lacking in sharpness, with a lack of awareness of the present moment—practice this simple exercise:

Tip your head forwards with your chin on your chest.
Then move your head upwards sharply, so that your chin is in the air.
The movement must be fairly quick and vigorous, but take care not to jar the neck.
Practise this movement three times and then return to your meditation.

This is a useful exercise as it can be performed quickly without disturbing your meditation position, and also will not disturb those around you if you are meditating with other people. Caution must be exercised with regard to jarring the neck, especially if you suffer from any problems with your neck. If so, practise the neck movement more slowly and smoothly.

16

Walking Meditation

The textiles classroom is long and thin and four large tables are arranged along the centre of the room. The lighting is subdued with only two of the strip lights being illuminated. A group of people have spaced themselves out around the tables, and are moving silently and extremely slowly. A single step takes half a minute to perform. The scene is dreamlike – as if life has switched into slow motion.

Physical practices—such as Indian or Tibetan yoga—are common in spiritual traditions and are an important aspect of meditation practice. Physical practice has several principles. On a purely practical level, physical exercise is essential during prolonged periods of meditation or else the body becomes stiff and loses condition. If one is engaged in a week of solitary retreat—for example—including long sessions of meditation where one is sitting very still, it is important to include sessions of exercise throughout the day. This will keep the body supple and free from problems with muscle and joint stiffness.

Physical practices are also often complete spiritual paths in themselves. When performed accurately such exercises can produce particular psycho-physical effects which then become the focus of meditation.

Walking Meditation is a simple physical method that can be used as a meditation in itself, or as an aid to meditation.

If you are starting to wish to meditate for longer periods of time, but are still finding sitting quite difficult, you may find it helpful to practice *Walking Meditation*. This can be used to break up a longer session of sitting meditation and release stiffness from the body. *Walking Meditation* is a method of *Letting Go* using the physical process of walking as the focus instead of the breath.

Meditation method 2 – *Walking Meditation*

Walk extremely slowly noticing each stage of the movement.
Observe raising the feet.
Observe the transfer of weight from one foot to the other and the balancing of the body.
Observe the sensation along the sole of the foot as you walk.
Observe the movement of hips, shoulders, legs.
Continue, walking as slowly and as mindfully as you can achieve.

You can keep your eyes gazing downwards with a soft focus a few metres ahead of you for this practice. Keep your legs flexed as you walk, and your centre of balance low.

It can be most enjoyable to practise this exercise in bare feet on a lawn in the summer, so that you can experience the delicious cool dampness of the grass beneath your feet. It is important to practise on a fairly level surface without obstacles, because maintaining balance can become difficult on uneven ground. If it is not practical to have bare feet or it is undesirable, it is best to wear flat shoes.

If practised correctly, it should take 30 seconds to a minute to complete a single step. The more slowly you can move, the more detail and subtlety of movement you will be able to detect. Continue with the movement for as long as you wish, and then return to your sitting practice.

I would not recommend that *Walking Meditation* should replace *Letting Go*. *Letting Go* should continue to be the primary and ground meditation, from which all other meditation practices become possible.

17

Om, A'a & Hung – Meditation Aid

The group have been meditating for ten minutes. A couple of people have started to fidget, and another appears to be studying one of the display boards rather than meditating. The tutor begins to sing, slowly intoning syllables for the length of an out-breath. The group join in and soon everyone looks focused once more and is able to sit still for the remaining few minutes of the session

The meditation aid in this chapter revisits the practice of singing *Om, A'a & Hung*, but this time as an aid to meditation. This practice will help if the mind is sleepy and dull, or if it is distracted and unfocused.

Meditation aid 2 – *singing Om, A'a and Hung*

(see figure 10-1 on page 54 for calligraphies of these syllables)

Sing the syllables Om, A'a and Hung in turn, using the same note and pitch. Sing each syllable for the length of an out-breath.
Sing the syllables over and over in turn.

Feel the vibration of Om at the forehead.
Feel the vibration of A'a at the throat.
Feel the vibration of Hung at the chest.

Feel the Om at the forehead resonating as white light.
Feel the A'a at the throat resonating as red light.
Feel the Hung at the chest resonating as blue light.

Continue with this practice until the mind feels more alert or more settled.

For this practice the eyes can be fully open, but they are *focused in space*. To be focused in space means that the eyes are in focus before you, but not focused on an object. They are focused in the space where an object could be, but as there is no object before you, they are simply focused in empty space.

The way to practise this is simple: extend your hand in front of you at arm's length and focus strongly on the tip of the index finger; notice what this feels like physically; then—without moving the eyes, or changing their focus—remove your hand. Your eyes are then focused on the space where your index finger had been, but no longer is – hence they are focused in that space. This exercise takes a little practice to accomplish, but you will soon get used to the experience of being focused in space rather than on an object. Gradually you will discover the point where it is easy to comfortably focus in space during your meditation session. If you have the opportunity to look at images of great historic Tibetan teachers, such as Padmasambhava or Milarépa, you may notice that their eyes are wide open and look slightly crossed. This is a depiction of them in meditation with their eyes focused in space.

18

Friend, Enemy, Stranger

"I've never thought about things like that before."

"No, nor me. I can see how I keep certain people in the 'not friend' category and never consider who they really are."

"I hadn't ever thought about how totally self-orientated my reactions to the people around me tend to be."

"It's fascinating to think that someone I don't like or someone I ignore, is another person's best friend. I guess I've always known this somehow, but never really brought it to the front of my mind to look at."

"It felt uplifting to feel more open-hearted towards the person I've been having a lot of trouble with at work, and then send them good energy. I'm sure this will help me get along with them better."

There are many different types of meditation. Some involve quietly sitting, some involve visualisation, some use the voice, and some engage the intellect in analysis. In this chapter we are going to look at a meditation that involves analytical contemplation and visualisation.

Analytical contemplation involves dwelling on a subject and attempting to deeply penetrate the essence of that subject in order to discover our preconceptions, our prejudices and our habitual views.

The meditation *Friend, Enemy, Stranger* looks at our concepts and feelings around people we like, people we do not get along with, and people with whom we have no personal connection.

In this meditation you will be choosing a friend, an enemy and a stranger to focus on as the subject matter of the practice. The 'friend' should be someone to whom you feel close, who you know well and care for. They could be a member of your family, a partner, or a dear friend. The 'enemy' should be someone who you dislike or find it difficult to get along with. 'Enemy' is quite a strong word and you may feel that you do not really have any enemies, in which case choose a person that you do not like spending time with, who seems to cause you problems, who you feel has unpleasant personal qualities, or who seems to dislike you. The 'stranger' should be someone you have seen in passing. It could be someone that you have said 'hello' to on occasion, or you see now and then in a shop or on your journey to work – but this should be a person about whom you know nothing personal. You do not know any details of their life or even anything about their personality.

Meditation method 3 – *Friend, Enemy, Stranger*

Sit in a comfortable meditation posture in a quiet room.

Begin with a short period of Letting Go.

Imagine that sitting in front of you are three people: a friend, an enemy and a stranger.

First of all bring your attention to your friend. Think about the factors that make you call this person 'friend'. What is it about them that you like? Why do you feel close to them? What points of contact are there in your lives that have developed into friendship and caring? Then think about them in general terms: think about their aspirations, needs and hopes. Contemplate on how they wish their loved ones to be healthy, safe and happy, on how they need to feel safe and happy themselves; how they wish to be free from painful situations in their lives, and wish to avoid unpleasantness. Consider that there are people in their lives—like you— who care about them and wish them to be comfortable and content. Continue to contemplate analytically in this way for some time focusing on the person you have chosen as your friend.

Then bring your attention to the person who you have chosen for the category of enemy. Think about the factors that make you dislike this person, or them dislike you – that might make you call them an 'enemy'. What is it about them that you dislike? Why do you feel wary of them? What points of contact are there in your lives that have developed into dislike and enmity? Then think about them in general terms: think about their aspirations, needs and hopes. Contemplate on how they wish their loved ones to be healthy, safe and happy, and how they need to feel safe and happy themselves; how they wish to be free from painful situations in their lives, and wish to avoid unpleasantness.

97

Consider that even though you do not like them or find them easy to be with, there are people in their lives who enjoy their company, and call them 'friend' – that for some people they would have been chosen for the 'friend' category for this meditation. Think about how there are people who care about them and wish them to be comfortable and content.

Continue to contemplate analytically in this way for some time focusing on your enemy.

Then bring your attention to the person who you have chosen as a stranger. Think about the factors which mean that you know very little about this person. Why is it that you have not got to know this person any better? Why do your lives glance off each other without really touching? Why are there so few points of contact in your lives?

Then think about them in general terms: although you know no personal details about this individual, you can confidently assume that they have aspirations, needs and hopes because they are a fellow human being. Contemplate on how you can know that they wish their loved ones to be healthy, safe and happy, and how they need to feel safe and happy themselves. Consider that there are people in their lives who care about them and wish them to be comfortable and content; how they wish to be free from painful situations in their lives, and wish to avoid unpleasantness. Consider that there are people in their lives who would consider them to be a dear friend.

Continue to contemplate analytically in this way for some time focusing on the person you have chosen as a stranger.

Having contemplated in this manner for some time, recognise yourself as the factor that creates the definition of friend, enemy or stranger. Recognise that these definitions are entirely dependent upon your perception and are not inherent definitions of these people in themselves.

Recognise your viewpoint of yourself at the centre of the stage of which the friend, enemy and stranger are peripheral players. Develop a sense of equanimity about these three people. See that—if circumstances were different—your enemy could become your friend, your friend could have been a stranger, your stranger could have been a friend, and so on. Look at all the possible permutations of relationships that could exist between you and these three people and understand that your view of them and the rôle that they play in your life is arbitrary and dependent upon circumstances. Continue to contemplate in this way from a perspective of equanimity.

Finish the analytical meditation session by celebrating your close relationship with your friend. Recognise the pleasure in that friendship and how it could be wonderful to feel that warmth and friendship towards everyone in your life.

Regret the difficulties in your relationship with your enemy and think about whether there is anything that you could do to change things – whether it might be possible to develop warmer feelings towards this person.

Finally think about the stranger. It may be that there cannot be any closer points of contact between you, but consider that it could be pleasant to respond in a more friendly way towards this person when your lives do cross.

The meditation *Friend, Enemy, Stranger* looks at our view of our lives, ourselves and other people. We can continually change the subjects of the meditation, choosing three different people at different times. Our view is the basis of all our expectations of life, our interpretations of circumstances, and our responses to the experiences we encounter in our lives. Our view governs how we are as people in the world and causes us to create an inter-penetrating network of reference points – that is, things that support our view of the way we think things are.

Whenever we encounter something new, we immediately try to compare it to something with which we are familiar: *this* is like *that*, *that* is like *this*; *that* person fits into the 'friend' category, but *this* person doesn't. We also judge everything: I like *this*, but I don't like *that*; *that* seems to support my comfort, but *this* seems to threaten it; *this* doesn't seem to impact on me at all, so I ignore it. This capacity to discriminate is a natural human function. We tend to allow it to govern us however, so that it becomes a dictatorship and we no longer encounter experiences directly and nakedly *as they are*.

This is a way in which we allow thought to rule our lives. We are so busy categorising our experience and trying to rationalise how it fits into the scheme of things, that we miss the opportunity to experience directly, nakedly, and in the present moment. The meditation *Friend, Enemy, Stranger* offers us an opportunity to look at our entrenched viewpoints. If we practise this meditation with a kindly intention and an open heart, it can become an inspiration to unlock our pre-packed, hermetically sealed, freeze-dried points of view.

Our enemy may never become our friend, but at least our view of them may become a little more balanced. We may be able to regard them as someone that *we* have a problem with, rather than as a person who *is* a problem. We can *own* our dislike and refrain from gathering other people to confirm our prejudice. We can avoid justifying our own unpleasantness. Perhaps we can feel a little warmer towards them – even if they continue to be unpleasant towards us.

It is important to take the understanding that has been discovered during this meditation practice out into our lives. This understanding needs to move beyond our meditation cushion to be a real experience. *Friend, Enemy, Stranger* has a 'feel good factor' that puts us in danger of becoming satisfied with the comfortable feeling of equanimity discovered through the practice. If we get up from our meditation cushion feeling we have done well but do not remember it in our everyday life, the experience never extends out into our life to make a difference to how we are in the world.

This meditation can actually make a difference to how we are in our lives and dissolve our fixed and rigid views. It can enable us to be kinder and more open, tolerant and more understanding. It may help us to recognise that others' apparent unkindness may be the result of ill health, confusion, or fear, so that we do not have to lock ourselves down in a bomb shelter of self-protective responses. It is a fact that smiling at people makes the world a happier place.

Recognising that all people are basically the same, with the same needs, hopes and aspirations, can help us avoid feeling threatened when those needs, hopes and aspirations have different flavours and qualities from our own. We can hold our own preferences lightly and enjoy the preferences of others – delighting in the endless array of personality and style of manifestation that human beings display.

Analytical meditation will be increasingly beneficial as your practice of *Letting Go* becomes more developed. The ability to focus and remain aware in the present moment through practising *Letting Go* will enhance your capacity to concentrate during analytical meditation and deeply penetrate the subject of your analysis.

If you find it difficult to remain focused during an analytical meditation, it may be that you need to spend more time practising *Letting Go* before moving on to other practices.

19

Loving Kindness

"I feel really good after that practice."
"Yes, so do I. I feel warm and happy inside."
*"I enjoyed visualising the golden light – it was most enriching
and invigorating."*

If our analytical meditation *Friend, Enemy, Stranger* has been clear
and penetrating and we have engaged with the practice with
openness and conviction, then the next meditation—*Loving
Kindness*—will follow on naturally. During the singing phase of
the practice, we can use the syllables *Om, A'a and Hung* that were
employed in the previous aid to meditation.

Meditation method 4 – *Loving Kindness*

Sit in a comfortable meditation posture in a quiet room.
Begin with a short period of Letting Go.
*Visualise in front of you a person, persons, or situation that you would like
to be able to help.*
Sing the yogic syllables Om, A'a and Hung over and over.
*As you sing, visualise golden light leaving your heart and filling those you
are visualising.*

Feel that you are giving warmth and friendship and a strong desire for them to be free from their unhappiness and discomfort.
Strongly feel a wish to help and benefit the persons or situation you are visualising, and believe that sending them golden light is of benefit.
Continue in this way for a little while until you see that the person, persons or situation you are visualising are filled with golden light. Feel content that you have really benefited them.

The subject of this meditation could be the friend, enemy and stranger of the previous practice, or it could be a friend or relative who is ill, a group of people whose cause you would like to help, or a situation you have heard about in the news that has moved you.

Having developed wisdom through our analysis of our view of a friend, an enemy and a stranger, our hearts spontaneously open with a wish to extend a kindly response to them. *Loving Kindness* is especially beneficial when practised immediately after *Friend, Enemy, Stranger*, because the opening and loosening of our view that we began with the analytical meditation can then be deepened into a wish to be kind and of benefit to our friend, our enemy and our stranger.

The two meditations practised together can really begin to change us through opening our self-orientated view and thereby inspiring the wish to be of help to others. We discover wisdom through analytical contemplation, and compassion arises through engaging with this more open view. Our experience of equanimity gives rise to the intention to be a kinder human being. *Loving Kindness* meditation can however, also be used as a complete practice on its own.

Loving Kindness meditation also has a 'feel good factor,' and we must take care that our wish to be kinder and to help others extends beyond our practice on our meditation cushion. These practices offer us a real opportunity to change ourselves and to be kinder and more aware human beings in our everyday interactions with others.

20

White A

The tutor demonstrates sounding the syllable A. Her breath extends for endless moments and finally dies away to silence. The energy in the room is potent in the silence that follows the sound of the syllable.

Meditation aid 3 – *Singing A*

For the length of a single, extended out-breath allow the sound A to arise as you breathe out.
Focus on the sound and the sensation of producing the sound.
Then return to your meditation.

This practice is useful as an antidote to sleepiness or distraction. It engages our energy and will wake us up if the mind is dull, or will clarify and settle the mind if it is lacking in focus.

A is the sound that naturally arises when we engage our vocal cords as we breath out. It is an uncontrived sound – we simply open our mouths and make noise and this is the sound that arises. Sound the *A* at whatever tone spontaneously occurs and at a volume and pitch that is comfortable and easy to perform.

As this meditation aid involves sound, it is best to use this only when practising alone. It may be distracting for others if you are meditating in a group.

The next aid uses the same syllable, but this time it is visualised as the focus for cutting through sleepiness or distraction. It will be necessary to have achieved some experience and success at visualisation before this practice will function as an aid to meditation.

Visualisation is more than simple imagination. Visualisation encompasses all the senses so that whatever is visualised is more than an imaginary image. There should be a felt sense of the object of visualisation actually appearing before you even if a clear image does not spontaneously arise.

Meditation aid 4 – *Visualisaing A*

Visualise a sphere of opalescent light.
Within the sphere is the white syllable A.
Focus strongly on the visualisation of the white syllable for a few minutes.
Feel the whiteness, purity and intensity of the syllable A.
Then let the visualisation dissolve and return to your meditation practice.

The Tibetan syllable A is illustrated in figure 20-1.

The sphere of light should be approximately the size of your closed fist and visualised a little above eye level in front of you. You may find it helpful to extend your arm in front of you with your hand in a fist, to get a sense of where the sphere should be and its size. The visualisation needs to be clear and vivid for this exercise to function as an aid to meditation.

These two practices—*Singing A* and *Visualising A*—can be combined to form one practice as an aid to meditation. The syllable A is visualised and also sounded at the same time.

figure 20-1 – White A
calligraphy by Ngakpa Chögyam

21

Thunderbolt Posture

A young woman, surrounded by several others, is balanced in an
elegant posture. Her arms begin to shake a little and then she
raises herself upwards slightly. With a gasp, she falls back onto
a pile of cushions, slightly red in the face and laughing.
The group of people around her are all smiling or laughing.
"Who wants to be next to try this?"

This chapter describes an aid to meditation called the *Thunderbolt*
Posture. Its principle is that of using extreme exertion for a very
short period of time in order to exhaust ourselves and propel us
into a moment of *mind without thought*. The purpose of the
posture is to exhaust ourselves in the shortest possible time. If
you have ever had to run flat out to catch a bus or a train, you
may have noticed that the state of breathless exhaustion such a
feat produces, allows a space of *mind without thought* to
spontaneously occur for a few moments. You leap onto the bus
at the very last moment as it is about to move off, and then the
driver asks you where you are going... but you find that your
mind is completely empty and you are not able to form any
concept of where you are or where you are going.

Such non-conceptual exhaustion cuts through sleepiness and distraction. It would not be very convenient to have to run far enough and fast enough however, to exhaust ourselves in this way as a method for cutting through sleepiness and distraction in our meditation practice.

Thunderbolt Posture achieves the same end in a matter of moments. The exercise takes less than a minute to perform.

The object of the posture is to make our bodies mirror the shape of the Thunderbolt Sceptre – a Buddhist ritual implement (see figure 21-1). The upper half of the shape is formed with the arms, and the lower half with the legs (figures 21-2 – 21-5). Before attempting this posture, check that you have sufficient room behind you to fall back onto, and that there is something soft to land on. Anyone with a heart condition, back or knee problems, or who is pregnant should avoid this practice. The exercise is strenuous, so if you have any concerns about your health, seek medical advice before trying it.

figure 21-1 – Thunderbolt Sceptre
line drawing by Khandro Déchen

Meditation aid 5 – *Thunderbolt Posture*

The arms:

Place your hands together approximately 5 cm above your head, with your fingers pointing vertically. Keep the palms of your hands touching throughout the exercise.

Attempt to make two contradictory movements at the same time: attempt to raise the hands higher vertically, whilst at the same time attempting to push the elbows backwards. Because these movements contradict each other, a lot of energy is created that cannot go anywhere, and the arms begin to judder.

The legs:

Now attempt to mirror with the legs the same shape that was made with the arms. Place the soles of the feet together and balance on the balls of your feet. Keep the knees wide apart and hanging downwards, and keep the back upright,

Once balanced, hold the starting position and place the arms in the overhead position and perform the contradictory movement of moving the hands upwards and the elbows backwards so that your arms start to judder.

Raise your body up by straightening your legs a little to the point that the bend in the knees is most difficult to maintain.

Completion:

Having held the position for a few seconds, collapse back onto the floor in a relaxed supine position with the arms and legs open.

Dwell in the space that has been created by performing the exercise.

Once you have recovered from the feeling of exhaustion, return to your meditation practice.

figure 21-2 – *Thunderbolt Posture*: starting position

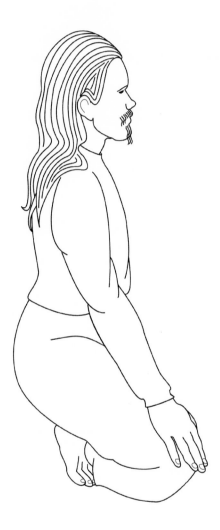

figure 21-3 – *Thunderbolt Posture*: starting position, side view

figure 21-4 – *Thunderbolt Posture*, full starting position

figure 21-5 – *Thunderbolt Posture:* final position

Practise the arms a little first until you experience the juddering of the energy in the arms, because this part of the exercise is easier to achieve than that of the legs. Adjust the feet as necessary to discover the starting position in which you can hold the balance. Ideally the soles of your feet should be together, but if you need to have your feet a little apart to achieve balance, this is fine. In order to get the knees to hang low and the back to be upright or leaning slightly backwards, the pelvis needs to be rotated.

How perfectly you can achieve the starting position will depend on your fitness and suppleness. The more fit and supple you are, the more perfectly you will need to perform the exercise in order to achieve its exhausting effect.

Remaining low when you raise the body makes it easy to stay balanced and you will be able to hold the posture too long. If you raise yourself up high so that the legs are straight, then again it becomes too easy to hold. If you can stay in the final position for more than a few seconds, then you are not performing the exercise accurately. As you raise the body up, you need to find the point that is most difficult to hold, so that you can literally only stay there for a few seconds of extreme effort.

It is essential to fall backwards rather than forwards after practising this posture. If you are tending to dive forwards, this is because your body is not sufficiently straight and vertical in the starting balance position.

When you collapse back onto the floor in the relaxed position your heart should be pounding, and you may feel breathless, but recovery should take no longer than it took to perform the exercise. *Thunderbolt Posture* is a short, sharp experience that cuts through dullness and discursive thought. I have found that people usually start to laugh when first presented with this exercise. It always produces some strong response – there is nothing mediocre or half-hearted about *Thunderbolt Posture*.

If using the exercise to help with sleepiness or distraction in meditation, it only needs to be performed once. *Thunderbolt Posture* is also an extremely useful practice if you suffer from insomnia, and in this instance it can be performed once, twice or three times.

22

Purification

In the centre of the chaotic room—with untidy piles of chairs, noticeboards covered with fabric samples and children's designs, and half-clothed mannequins lurking in one corner—sit a group of people arranged in a half circle. In front of them, propped on a chair, is an image of a beautiful woman. Her skin is pure white and she is naked apart from ornaments carved from bone. One of the group of meditators sings a lyrical melody. Some stare at the image of the woman, some have their eyes closed. The atmosphere in the room is peaceful and vibrant.

Through meditation we may discover that there are qualities and aspects of our lives that are not as we would wish them to be. We may recognise that sometimes we cause others pain through our lack of tact or our insensitivity. We may feel that we could be *more* than we are – kinder, cleverer, wiser, more appreciative, more generous. When we begin to establish a daily practice of meditation, it often seems that our shortcomings are suddenly brought into stark relief. It seems as if we are becoming less tolerant and more irritable, less aware and more insensitive, less warm and more critical – whereas in fact we are simply noticing traits that have always been there.

From recognition of these undesirable qualities, the wish may arise to dissolve these aspects of our personality. Purification practice arises through the recognition of the wish to free ourselves from the patterns in our lives that cause us to hurt ourselves and others. It offers the possibility of cleansing ourselves through visualisation. In our meditation practice we can work on dissolving the unhelpful, unskilful, neurotic patterns that we notice in ourselves, and invite in awareness, so that we embrace more helpful, skilful and enlightened attitudes and conduct.

Meditation method 5 – *Purification*

Sit in a comfortable meditation posture in a quiet room.
Begin with a short period of Letting Go.
In front of you have an image of a person or being who you regard as gentle, wise and kind – someone you would aspire to be like.
Visualise that this person or being is in front of you and above you – that they have appeared before you.
Focusing on your in-breath, visualise breathing in light that radiates from the heart of your visualised being. Visualise that this light enters your body through the top of your head, and floods into your body filling you with the cleansing light.
Continue in this way until you feel that you are filled with light.
Switch your focus to the out-breath, and as you breathe out visualise smoke pouring out of you through the base of your torso.
Continue in this way for some time, feeling that all negativity, illness, ill will and neurosis is leaving your body and your mind as you breathe out the visualised smoke.

*After a while feel that all negativity and unwanted neurotic patterns have
been breathed away and you remain filled with light.*
Dwell for a few moments in the experience of purity of body and mind.

The person visualised could be an actual person you admire, a
religious figure or an abstract being. If you prefer not to use the
image of a person, you can visualise a sphere of light instead.
Visualise this sphere about the size of your fist and above your
head, emitting the light that pours into you.

When practising purification, I have before me an image of
Yeshé Tsogyel – the female tantric Buddha (figure 22-1).
During the two phases of the practice—receiving the light, and
breathing out smoke—I sing her awareness song. When
practising this alone, you can simply engage in the visualisation
as described above without singing. Alternatively, you can sing
the three syllables *Om, A'a* and *Hung*, described earlier, during
the two phases of the practice – when breathing in light, and
when breathing out smoke.

Purification is an energetic practice that transforms us in an
energetic manner. It involves the movement of energy through
visualisation. This practice has at its core an acknowledgement
of our innate goodness – our naturally existent capacity to be
kind and wise. It would not be possible for us to experience any
benefit from the practice of purification if innate goodness was
not naturally self-existent. This could be compared to a healthy
person wishing to get physically fit. The unfit body engages in
keep fit practices, and gradually the body becomes fitter.
The potential to have a fit body is always present in a healthy
person who is unfit.

123

figure 22-1 Yeshé Tsogyel
line drawing by Khandro Déchen

Purification is another practice that I describe as having a 'feel good factor.' It is important not to let this 'feel good factor' go to our heads when we use this method. Purification practice *can* make us kinder and more considerate human beings if we practise it regularly with awareness and kindly intention. We are not automatically purer beings however, simply through engaging in this practice. We still have to live our lives with the intention of being kind and considerate people on a moment-by-moment basis.

The measure of one's purity is in the capacity to be kind and sensitive, to be willing to put ourselves out to help others, and to respect and appreciate the lifestyle and opinions of others in the real world. There is no purpose in being able to experience oneself as radiating pure light and have an intense experience of purity whilst sitting on one's meditation cushion, if one cannot display down-to-earth patience, tolerance and respect of others in ordinary life situations. Purification is a powerful practice and a useful method, but it must be supported by real, human, kindly activity. The power of the meditation experience must follow through into the way we live our lives.

23

Exchange

"It was wonderful to feel that I could take away my friend's illness. I know he would feel good about me visualising his illness dissolving."

The practice of purification can—if wished—be followed immediately by the practice of *Exchange*. Once we have purified ourselves, we are able to be of benefit to others. Once we experience the happiness that arises through discovering equanimity and a loving heart, we will naturally and spontaneously wish others to share this experience.

Meditation method 6 – *Exchange*

Begin with the purification practice.

Then visualise someone who has a problem or illness and who you would like to help. Visualise their problem or illness as smoke.

Begin to sing the syllables again, visualising as you do so that you are drawing the smoke of the person's illness or difficulties out of them and are taking it into yourself as you sing.

Take in the smoke of their suffering and neutralise it through the power of your visualisation of light. Carry on visualising that you are taking away all their problems and unhappiness. Really believe that you have relieved them of their distress and misfortune and feel satisfied and content.

Practices of exchange should not be regarded as martyrdom. We are not sitting on our cushion at the end of our practice feeling wretched and unappreciated, having taken on the suffering of the world. We are not frightened of what we have taken from other beings. This is not the point of the practice at all. *Exchange* is an expression of heroism, boldness and audacity.

There is no need to feel concern that you *are* taking on the suffering of those visualised. You are not going to contract your friend's cancer, or experience a catastrophe like an earthquake, or find yourself suffering starvation through engaging in this practice. You may benefit innumerable people however, by becoming kinder and more open-hearted through practising this visualisation because of the effect it has upon your view of yourself and others.

24

Fruit of Meditation

It is the first time that the group have been asked to sit together for a period of twenty minutes. The room is quiet and peaceful, with an atmosphere of relaxed concentration. Occasionally a person may jerk their head upwards three times — employing the aid for sleepiness; or someone may adjust their position. Otherwise all members of the group are completely still, with their eyes gazing downwards, relaxed and comfortable in their practice.

The practise of *Letting Go* develops awareness. It also develops a sense of spaciousness in the mind and the capacity to observe thought rather than being overwhelmed by involvement with its content. Increased awareness enables us to become kinder human beings because we are no longer at the mercy of our automatic responses. Through developing space in the mind, we discover space in our reactivity. We find that we have choice about how we interact with others and how we engage with the circumstances of our lives.

The choice of the words *'Letting Go'* is particular in describing this meditation practice. The phrase *letting go* successfully encompasses the nature of the practice. We *'let go'* of thought.

We do not attempt to force thought out of the mind. We do not regard thought as meaningless or bad – it is just that the practice is to *let it go*. We let go of thought in order to discover what happens when we are not encouraging and entertaining thought.

What am I like when I am not thinking, classifying, checking things out, worrying, planning, fantasising...? Who am I when I am no longer thinking all the time and defining myself through those thought patterns...? What is it like to experience my mind when it is still, without thought...? The answer to these questions can be discovered through the practice of *Letting Go*.

This practice however, is not to be understood as mental liposuction – we are not draining out the unwanted, fatty content of the mind as an ultimate aim, in order to discover a fat-free, slim-line, permanent state of empty mind. We shall need that fatty material to burn later on as the fuel to transform our experience of ourselves. We can only begin to do this however, once we have experienced what we are like when the continual chatter of our minds has subsided. We can only use thought effectively when we are able to actually be truly aware of it – when we can discover its quality and movement as well as its content. Through allowing thought—the intellectual, cognitive aspect of mind—to settle we reveal its basis and nature, and discover the state of *mind without thought*.

We could use an analogy here to help us understand this view of the mind. Our usual experience of the mind is like the waves on the ocean. They swell up and then break and disappear. Our thoughts are like this.

130

There is also the vast body of water however, that is the ocean from which the waves are born and which is not affected in its vastness by the transient swelling and breaking of waves. This vast ocean is the basic or fundamental mind of which we usually have little experience and which we are seeking to discover through meditation.

The experience of *mind without thought* is the fruit that we are seeking to discover through the practice of *Letting Go*. This is the state where thought is no longer arising in the mind and we are alert, focused and present. To be present means that one is awake and aware of whatever is happening—or not happening —now, in the present moment. This is not a withdrawn or 'other-worldly' state of being. It is vibrant, clear and in the here and now. The mind is alert and sensitive to all sensory experiences, but they do not disturb the state of dwelling in *mind without thought*. When thought is no longer arising we find that there is space and emptiness of mind. The mind is bright and alert, but there is no conceptual content – there is no thought-story playing out, memory being revisited, or plan being envisioned. There is no commentary running through the mind, commenting on our experience. The mind is empty – but this is not a vacant, 'no-one home' type of emptiness. It is more like a pregnant pause – a state of potency where movement could spontaneously arise, or emptiness could continue.

A custom of meditation practice for ten minutes a day, will start to produce noticeable results within approximately three months for most people, if practice is consistent and committed.

Moments, or short periods, of *mind without thought* will start to occur. At first we may feel discomfited or excited when such moments begin to occur, and immediately fill them with thought again. Gradually however, we will get used to the quiet space of *mind without thought*. We may then be surprised to find that it can be quite easy to remain with stillness in the mind without thought arising, and with a sense of vibrant alertness – in a state of stabilised emptiness. It will start to feel comfortable to dwell in this alert, awake condition.

Letting Go of thought and discovering *mind without thought*, exposes the habit of using thought as a conduit through which we experience everything in our lives. We will start to notice our own habit patterns. Over time we will start to become aware of the triggers to those habit patterns. Eventually we will start to realise that we have a choice about whether or not we engage with a habit pattern. We will find that our habitual response seems to click in ever so slightly more slowly and our patterns become more transparent.

At first it may seem that we are becoming more irritable and less tolerant. It may seem that we are less pleasant people than we had thought ourselves to be, and we may become distressed on finding that we are not as kind, patient and gentle as we would like to be. But it is not that we *have* become less pleasant – it is just that we are noticing how we really are for the first time. We are seeing ourselves being territorial and irritable, self-centred and paranoid, and bewildered or indifferent to the needs of others as if for the first time.

We have always been that way, but our meditation practice has revealed our habit patterns and self-protective strategies. We discover the moment of choice between the emotional trigger and the emotional response. We discover the moment of choice between the arising of the cutting retort and its voicing; the awareness of an habitual opinion and its expression.

We will lose the entrenched view of ourselves as central, and others as peripheral. We are able to respond in a more open and fluid manner. Through continuing to practice meditation, this awareness will deepen and our capacity to let go of unhelpful habit patterns will increase. This, in itself, brings about a degree of relaxation.

Letting Go enables us to become less engrossed in thought so that we discover the ability to experience nakedly and directly. Conceptual definitions—about our character and personality, our emotions, the people we meet, our lifestyle, the way we dress, our political opinion—no longer rule our lives. Definition, opinion, prejudice and preconception no longer dominate our interaction with others and our world.

Letting Go in meditation gradually extends out into our everyday life so that we begin to be able to let go of the process of *doing us.* We no longer rely on definitions, opinions and preconceptions as reference points to support the '*me project*' where we are the centre of the universe. We start to realise that there is a subtle level of mind that can be discovered which will expand our view and open out our experience of ourselves, others and our environment.

133

We do not own our minds. We do not have any real understanding or control over our minds. We can all remember a time when we found that we could not stop thinking about something however much we wanted to; or a time when we could not get to sleep because of the mind's thought processes running wild. We are rarely—if ever—simply quiet with ourselves. If quiet space does arise spontaneously, we fill it. If our life is quiet we fill the quietness with music, television, a hobby, work and social interaction. People nowadays seek entertainment even when they are out cycling or walking in the park. Increasingly we enclose ourselves in a separate world plugged into headphones, rather than hearing the sounds of what is around us. If our mind is quiet we fill it with memories, conversations we wish we had had, plans, going over old hurts, imagining problems or dwelling on problems, fantasies and day dreams. We are fixated and fascinated by thought. While we have little or no experience of who we are or what our existence is like, except through the filter of this perpetual conceptual noise, we cannot enter into examining our relationship with thought and discover its qualities.

By letting go of thought we can discover the space of *mind without thought*. Through *Letting Go* the arising and dissolving of conceptual mind can be revealed as a wave that surges and breaks on the surface of the deep, still ocean of fundamental mind. Through discovering the quietness of fundamental mind we can gain direct experience of who we are, what we are and where we are, rather than trying to discover this through the ebb and flow of concept.

By learning to access and be comfortable in the space of *mind without thought*, our relationship with thought can change. Through this change our relationship with all the senses and with our emotions can also be transformed.

Mind without thought is the experience of empty mind. Our usual experiences of emptiness can be disconcerting and uncomfortable, so it is helpful to become accustomed to this experience in our meditation practice in order to find emptiness less threatening when it naturally occurs. We experience emptiness in our lives when we are stripped of points of reference. These points of reference may be in connection with our job, our relationship, our parents, our hobby, our home, our habits – anything that provides some definition of who we are and our place in the world. If our life circumstances bring chaos into the neat organisation of the factors that provide definition in our lives—through loss, lack of success, change, and unexpected occurrences—we may feel insecure, threatened, isolated, anxious and bewildered.

The experience of emptiness through changing circumstances may be welcome or unwelcome, but both can be unsettling through the effect they create in our lives. We may be made redundant or gain a promotion; we may lose our partner or start a new relationship; we may be evicted or move house; our favourite club may close or we decide to take up a new interest – all of these situations can change our ordinary routines and disrupt our habits so that we feel a lack of familiar reference points. This is an experience of emptiness.

Losing reference points can make us feel insecure. Our reaction to feeling insecure can tend to be to establish reference points again as quickly as possible. That is, we categorise and evaluate new experience in terms of past experience so that it feels more manageable. We do not like to stay in the state of not-knowing, of the unfamiliar or ambivalent. The tool that we use to categorise and evaluate, and to re-establish reference points, is the intellect, or thought. By rationalising new experience into categories based on past experience however, we miss the opportunity to experience nakedly and directly.

Once we have established a regular meditation practice and started to get used to the experience of emptiness through discovering *mind without thought*, we find that we feel less threatened by change and emptiness when it arises in our lives. We let go of immediately grasping for reference points or indulging unhelpful emotional states. Our meditation practice enables us to dwell in the state of lack of reference more comfortably, and we do not need to immediately grasp for old, familiar habit patterns. We start to engage with experience more directly and feel comfortable with that directness.

Letting Go is a simple practice, but it takes effort and conscientious commitment to achieve results. *Letting Go* is a practice that requires perseverance. We are so accustomed to our minds being filled with thought, that it takes considerable application to the method to allow ourselves to let thought go. We find that we are so accustomed to a mind full of discursive thought that it is really quite difficult to allow this perpetual chatter to subside.

Sometimes absolute beginners do experience surprising moments of *mind without thought* quite quickly, but then they may find such moments just as suddenly disappear. Practice, and the fruits of practice, are not linear. We will have days when our mind is quite clear and still, and we will have days when thought is an endless, continuous, and highly involved process that will not dissolve.

Many of us find the process of meditation quite relaxing initially because it is a new and different experience. We find that simply sitting and allowing ourselves to disengage from the ordinary activities of life produces a still peacefulness. Once we have become accustomed to this initial novelty however, effort is then required to continue with the meditation practice and develop awareness. The effort required to continue practising *Letting Go* can be challenging, as inevitably we will experience the frustrations that arise whenever we apply ourselves to a new activity. We could become discouraged on discovering that letting go of thought is not easy.

Beginning any new activity is a mixture of excitement and disappointment – excitement at observing progress, and disappointment that progress is slow. If we begin learning to play the guitar—for example—we may be inspired and enthusiastic when we successfully produce a pleasant sound; but we may be frustrated and disheartened when we find that our fingers will not form the shape of a new chord and the sound does not ring purely. If we continue to practise regularly however, we can be sure that our guitar playing will improve.

Undoubtedly we will continue to experience difficulties and setbacks, but our capacity to play the guitar will gradually increase. It is exactly the same with meditation – if we practise our capacity will increase.

Some people assume that meditation is a 'natural' activity, and that because it is a 'natural' activity it will therefore be easy and require little application and effort. Although it is true that a meditative state of mind is our natural condition, we do not dwell in this natural condition and therefore have to apply effort to discover it. If we fail to understand the need to continue to apply ourselves to the method we may find that our meditation sessions have lapsed into periods of day dreaming. We rest in a cosy, woolly, inner world, where the mind is allowed to drift like cotton wool through the vagaries of conceptual mind – no longer really dwelling on thought, but also not truly letting it go.

There is no harm in spending some time every day quietly day dreaming in the world of our own mind – and it may be enjoyable if habitually we never stop being active long enough to just sit still and do nothing. Day dreaming is not the principle of meditation however, and settling for this in the belief that it *is* meditation practice will mean that the benefits of *Letting* Go will be missed. Woolly, cosy day dreaming will not offer the quality of relaxation that can be found through discovering spaciousness in the mind, and eventually—or in times of crisis— it will be found that the relaxation gained from day dreaming is of no real value in helping dissolve the habitual thought patterns that create stress and emotional conflict.

Day dreaming is not conducive to discovering *mind without thought*, and the nature of this empty state may be misunderstood through believing that day dreaming is meditation. In *Letting Go* we are not aiming for a dampened down, thought-suppressed state. *Mind without thought* is a vibrant, creative state of awareness. It is vivid with an electric sense of being awake in the present moment. Even momentary glimpses of this vibrant state will begin to open our experience of ourselves so that we find our lives are less stressful, we are happier and more relaxed.

Discovering our habitual patterns through the practice of *Letting Go* will change us. Our experience of ourselves and our relationship with ourselves and our world, will start to change. Glimpses of change and of the potential for transformation that meditation offers can also be challenging. Initial glimpses of *mind without thought* can be startling. We may suddenly feel that this new and exciting path of self discovery and self awareness is a more profound experience than we had anticipated. We may feel that it is pushing the boundaries of our comfort zone. Any new venture that we enter into will inevitably create changes in us however, through our contact with new ideas and people. Such transformation can especially be expected when we venture into meditation practice.

Most of us are afraid of change to some extent, even when we seek out life-changing experiences. It is as if we want to watch ourselves learning to be different people from a safe distance. We wish to become more peaceful and have a deeper understanding of ourselves – but we want to experience it as an observer so that we can check that it is safe.

Alternatively we wish to engage with experiences that challenge us, open our minds and stretch our limited view – but we wish to retain all our comfortable old habit patterns at the same time. The shiny new boots that will enable us to traverse the path of practice are so fancy and inviting. There is the intricate pattern of their tooling and the silky smoothness of the leather. The smell of leather and polish is intoxicating – but our sloppy old slippers are so very safe and comfortable. An expansive view can be discovered through meditation practice, but we have to let go of our certainty about our habitual views and opinions in order to embrace it

As well as being the primary meditation practice, *Letting Go* is also the starting point for all other meditation methods. It is essential to develop some experience of *Letting Go* in order to be able to apply oneself fully to other meditation methods.

The practice of *Letting Go* is the basis for the development of awareness and concentration. With sufficient awareness we can gain an understanding of the nature of our experience. With sufficient concentration we can apply ourselves to any technique. Through developing awareness and concentration it is possible to fully grasp the principle and function of meditation methods and achieve true relaxation.

The certainty of practice changing us is also true of practices of visualisation. Visualisation opens a door to the experience of ourselves as more than material beings existing in a material world. The practice of visualisation is *of itself* transformative.

Purification practice—for example—works with our energetic being through visualisation. It is the discovery of our own innate purity. It will alter our view of ourselves and others, of our internal environment and our external environment.

We are not creating purity, we are discovering it. It is the activation of our natural capacity to be pure. Through becoming aware of our innate purity and visualising that purity, we discover the reality of its existence. Ultimately we realise that purification practice is irrelevant because purity *is* our natural condition. While we experience a gap between how we would like to be and how we see that we are however, purification is a worthwhile and powerful practice that can help us move towards discovering our innate purity.

The *Friend, Enemy, Stranger* meditation *Loving Kindness* and *Exchange* also work with our view of ourselves and others. They can work towards the development of a less *me-centric* attitude, so that we become less belligerent about our opinions, less prejudiced about our viewpoints, and more fluid in relationship to others.

I think Mrs Jones is a nasty person, but Mr Jones thinks she is the most wonderful and kind person in the world. Neither of these views is right or wrong and neither is true. They are simply different, based on differing experiences and relationships. These views are therefore empty of inherent reality. One is my opinion and the other is Mr Jones's opinion. When we realise that neither opinion is a truth, we can start to hold our opinion lightly and be open to entertaining the alternative view. This makes everything much more spacious and light-hearted – even amusing.

141

The same approach can be applied to ourselves, so that we catch a glimpse of the lack of an inherent self.

I think I am Nor'dzin – a middle-aged woman who actually feels inside more like thirty-something. I am overweight and sometimes a bit slow and lazy, and I can be rather irritable.

My one son thinks I am a nice size and did not like it when I lost a lot of weight because I became bony and less cuddly. My other son says I work all the time, too much and too hard, and am always dashing about. Some people say I am a patient and tolerant person.

These opinions of Nor'dzin are incompatible – they contradict one another, so they are not 'truth'. They are partial truths. The 'real' Nor'dzin is a continuous stream of changing definitions, emotions, and mind-states. The self that we think of as being so solid and permanent, so separate from others, so continuous and defined, starts to look less certain.

Practising *Letting Go* offers insight into the emptiness of self through observing and letting go of the flow of thought, and learning to dwell in the present moment with awareness.

Practices such as *Friend, Enemy, Stranger* loosen our certainty about the reality of our views and opinions, so that our relationship with these becomes more spacious. We start to see that reality does not quite exist as we think it exists, and is in fact dependent upon our view of it. Our understanding of the people in our lives is based on how those people relate to *me*, and how *I* have judged them, and the assumptions *I* have made about them.

Once we start to experience this awakening of a more loose and spacious view, we can start to interact with people more directly and openly. We can avoid responding to them based on previous experience, prejudice and interpretation of our perception of them. Through feeling less certain of our self definitions we can start to feel less self-protective, and invest less energy into supporting and maintaining a view of ourselves.

We all learn to some extent to flow between differing definitions of ourselves – here I am mother, here I am daughter, here I am wife, here I am student, here I am teacher, here I am boss, here I am subordinate... ad infinitum. An inability to move between differing self-definitions can create a great deal of unhappiness for ourselves and others – I will upset my mother if I am condescendingly maternal towards her; I may create conflict and confusion at work if I behave in an overly familiar manner with my subordinates; I will be unable to learn from my teacher if I approach them like a teacher instead of as a student; my relationship will be unsatisfactory if I behave like a child with my partner rather than as an adult spouse.

Loving Kindness meditation explores the development of a kind and open heart. Through practising *Friend, Enemy, Stranger,* we begin to understand that potentially everyone could be our friend – or at least looked upon with a kindly eye. Through engaging with developing our view in this way in meditation, it will start to occur to us that we could feel kindly towards the people we meet who appear to us to be an enemy or a stranger in the moment that we encounter them.

Through visualising giving away our own feelings of happiness to the irritating woman at work; or to the chap who cut us up on the motorway; or to the children who hang around noisily outside our house; or to the bus driver who did not wait for us; or to the cat that keeps defæcating in our flowerbeds; or to the wasps that have set up home in our shed... we open ourselves to the possibility of having a friendly relationship with everyone and everything everywhere.

It is important to have a balanced view of what effect our visualisation practice has had upon us however, and not to get carried away by the 'feel good factor' of these practices. If we find that we have insufficient tolerance to refrain from the hurtful remark; if we lack awareness of the pain our insensitivity causes another; or if we continue to allow ourselves to become irritated by other people's style of living when it differs from ours – then our development of equanimity and our *Loving Kindness* meditation has not been of real benefit to us in terms of changing how we are as human beings in the world.

Sitting on our meditation cushion visualising helping and benefiting others has not been sufficient for real development of our view if we find ourselves unable to be simply kind to others in ordinary, everyday situations. There *are* benefits to prayer, kindly wishes and expressions of goodwill, but these need to be followed through with actual kindly activity and real work for the benefit of others.

Changing the world involves changing ourselves, and *Loving Kindness* meditation is an opportunity to effect such change. The *only* way to change the world is to change ourselves.

We will know that we are being successful in becoming kinder people when we find that we are less irritable, more aware and open to others' needs, and less focused on our own needs.

The changes in our lives that should occur through engaging in practices such as the *Loving Kindness* meditation, are not particularly about becoming a campaigner for world peace, volunteering at our local charity shop, or giving up our day off to help out at the hostel for the homeless – although these are all worthy causes in themselves. It is more about how we change in our relationship to the person we find next to us in any moment of our day – whether we have time for that person; are friendly, respectful and considerate to them; whether we let go of our prejudices and preconceptions; whether we can be decent, honourable and kind people in every aspect of our lives. This is the level at which change needs to happen, rather than in some grand gesture or overt charitable act.

If we are able to change in the moment and be a better human being to whomever we are with in that moment – then this will ripple outwards and really change the world.

We may also find that sometimes we experience the opposite to the 'feel good factor.' Through analytical meditation, visualisation and *Letting Go*, our awareness of how we really are in the world increases. We will then start to notice when we are thoughtless or unkind, when the habitual response clicked in before we became aware of it. It is important not to become discouraged or irritated when such awareness of ourselves arises.

We must celebrate the increased awareness and forgive ourselves for our inability to follow through and avoid the habitual response. Gradually more and more space will develop in our minds as we continue to practise. Then we will start to discover the moment of time in which it is possible to let go of the habitual response that arises, and respond in a more helpful and kind way through the awareness in that moment.

Singing the syllable *A* and syllables *Om, A'a & Hung* can be experienced as meditation practices in their own right when we have gained some experience of meditation – they become *Meditational Song*. Meditational Song continues the journey of deepening awareness. Through allowing ourselves to enter the dimension of sound, we are also letting go of thought, and hence supporting and strengthening our practice of *Letting Go*.

For many people discovering the joy of singing is in itself a transformative experience. If in the past they have rarely allowed themselves to freely open their voices, it is liberating to be given permission to make as much noise as they wish. People can grow in confidence and feelings of self-worth through this practice. Singing is also particularly useful for helping with emotional states. If you are experiencing a lot of emotional problems in your life, Meditational Song may be a most beneficial supportive practice for a while if you are finding that your mind tends to go over and over your problems when you are practising *Letting Go*. Song can help us to engage with the energy of emotional states in a creative manner.

There are three ways that we usually engage with emotion: we express it, we suppress it, or we dissipate it.

An example of expressing emotion would be to engage in a heated argument, perhaps saying hurtful things that we regret later. Suppressing emotion means that we do not allow it any expression, which can lead to feelings of resentment and inner anger. We dissipate emotion by immersing ourselves in some physical activity or by entertaining ourselves, so that the emotional state gradually subsides through distracting ourselves from it.

Through engaging with Meditational Song in times of emotional turmoil—singing *A*, or *Om, A'a & Hung*—we can harness the energy of the emotion in a creative manner and allow it to feed our practice. We sing the emotion and immerse ourselves in the experience of our voice and the sound. In this way we can avoid the pitfalls of expression and suppression that can be harmful to others and ourselves.

It is wise to recognise when *Letting Go* is not possible – when there is so much turmoil in our lives that it tends to surface too strongly and too painfully when we meditate. At such times analytical meditation or visualisation may be easier practices to apply, or it may be that a relaxation technique or breathing exercise is more appropriate.

It is still advisable however, to maintain the intention to continue with the commitment of practising *Letting Go* every day. We have to continue with this whatever the state of our mind or whatever the chaos of our lives. If we do not, we run the risk of allowing our emotions and our life circumstances to become an excuse for lack of practice.

I am ill today, so I won't do my practice... I am too tired today, so I'll leave practice till tomorrow... I am too distressed today, so I'll leave it and practise more tomorrow when I feel better... I am so busy today, I don't have time for practice...

Although we may indeed be ill, tired, distressed or swamped with life, it is better to sit and attempt to engage with meditation practice than to let our daily commitment lapse. We begin with the practice of *Letting Go* as usual whatever our state of mind, or whatever life circumstances we are experiencing. Then, if we find that we are totally unable to succeed in letting go of thought or churned up emotion, we can sing or use a breathing exercise or relaxation technique – but at least we have succeeded in maintaining the continuity of engaging with *Letting Go*.

If we carry on in this way, skilfully using meditation methods, breathing exercises and relaxation techniques as a range of tools in our toolbox, we can pull out the best practice to support our ground practice of *Letting Go*. If we continue in this way greater awareness will develop. Through this it is certain that we will discover the capacity to be kinder and more honourable human beings, living our lives with integrity.

Learning to be fearless and at ease in the empty space of the mind—*mind without thought*—enables us to be fearless and at ease when our life circumstances thrust us into moments of emptiness. Through being less anxious and more comfortable with ourselves, we are able to be more tolerant and appreciative of other people, and with the situations in life that we encounter day-by-day. We discover open appreciation and enjoyment and awaken to our natural state of relaxation.

Author's Note

To gain benefit from any technique, exercise or method that we are taught, it is necessary to have confidence in the teacher. It is necessary to enter the dimension of the teacher's view so that we can engage with the material that is being taught. We also need to have confidence in the source of the material they are offering – that it arises from tried and tested practices that have been practised and understood by the teacher. In Buddhism the source of practice is the spiritual tradition, and the teacher is the means of conveying the teachings of that spiritual tradition. Fully engaging with a teacher and spiritual tradition provides tremendous focus and energy for progress in practice.

The necessity for confidence in the teacher is true in any sphere of study – such as learning how to play a musical instrument, horse riding, badminton, painting, or learning a new language. If our music teacher tells us that we need to practice scales every week in order to develop our skill, but we ignore this instruction and never do so – we cannot then be surprised when we fail to make progress. If my riding instructor tells me that I will be more secure in the saddle if I lengthen my leg and keep my heels down, I should not then be surprised at falling off the horse when I curl up into foetal position when the horse spooks.

If we apply ourselves seriously to meditation practice, experiences such as *meditation phenomena* will arise, plus an increasing awareness of how the mind functions.

Meditation phenomena can be delightful, but they can also be unsettling, and are often confusing. They can arise through any of the senses or conceptually. When I first began to meditate I used to experience a strange physiological meditation phenomenon. I was practising with my eyes closed and would feel that my body was leaning over to one side at an angle of 45°. I would open my eyes, only to discover that in fact I was still sitting perfectly upright.

This was a fairly mild and innocuous meditation phenomenon, but people can have more extraordinary experiences which can be pleasant, unpleasant, or peculiar. If we do not have a guide to ask about such experiences we can become distracted by them. We may believe that the meditation phenomenon itself is a great spiritual achievement to be dwelt upon and sought out when it does not spontaneously arise. The danger then is that we become a seeker of meditation phenomena or a meditator upon these phenomena – and the actual purpose and focus of our meditation practice is lost. Meditation phenomena can be observed, even enjoyed – but then we let them go.

If we embrace meditation practice as a long term commitment our capacity to self-advise will eventually be exhausted. It will then become necessary to seek out a teacher with meditation experience who can answer our questions, help us with difficulties and obstacles that arise, and guide us to further development of our meditation practice.

Learning how to play a musical instrument on one's own may lead to a degree of proficiency and familiarity with the instrument. To become a virtuoso however, it will be necessary to receive instruction from an accomplished player, and to make music with other musicians. Similarly meditation practice will be of more benefit in the context of learning from a teacher and shared experience with other practitioners.

Practising meditation on your own with only yourself as a guide could be compared to wearing away a rock with water from a gentle stream – the water *will* erode the rock, but it will take a long time to have any great effect and the effect may lack focus. Becoming part of a spiritual tradition and working with a teacher is like turning our gentle stream of spiritual practice into a powerful, focused torrent that will quickly cut through the mountain of our mental distortions and neurotic mind-states.

Without a spiritual guide we always remain the controller of our experience. *We* can decide on the practices we like and ignore those we do not like. *We* can decide which meditation phenomena are significant and which are not. *We* can push ourselves too hard or be too soft on ourselves. As the governors of our own practice we lack an overview – we cannot see where our practice could be adjusted to deepen and develop our understanding and experience.

This book is an introduction to meditation practice. It introduces a range of methods to explore for someone wishing to learn about meditation. Its object is to take the reader on a journey of preparation through relaxation techniques and breathing exercises, and to introduce basic meditation practices.

It offers a starting point for those who are seeking information, so that some experience of meditation can be gained as a basis for further exploration of such practices.

The meditation practices in this book have their basis in Buddhism. It is possible to practise these methods without being a Buddhist or having an interest in Buddhism, but long term practice will inspire experiences that it may be difficult to understand from a rational, intellectual perspective outside of a spiritual tradition.

In Buddhism our confused and neurotic condition is often compared to being asleep – because our relationship with reality is more like being in a dream than being awake. We lack awareness because of our habitual patterns so that we are like confused and unresponsive sleepwalkers.

To wake up and truly discover complete wakefulness our meditation practice needs the guidance and focus of a teacher and a spiritual tradition. Hence I would urge anyone who establishes a long term, committed, daily practice of meditation to seek a teacher and a meditation tradition. Once your meditation practice is established a personal teacher, who has travelled the path before you, will be able to guide you to further exploration on the journey.

Ngakma Nor'dzin

July 2010, Cardiff, Wales

Appendices

Making Sitting Equipment

Cushions & a Sitting Strap

Appendix A

Rectangular Cushion

Use a strong fabric to make your cushions covers, such as cotton drill, denim or upholstery fabric. The material should not be slippery and needs to be tough and hard-wearing. Cushions intended for meditation practice are often made in muted colours, such as black or maroon.

This rectangular cushion is ideal for sitting as it provides sufficient height for the sitter's knees to hang lower than their hips. It consists of a dense block of foam covered in a material cover. The height should be at least 15cm. The width and depth can be adjusted to suit your personal preference, but approximately 45cm by 30cm. You will also need a zip 2cm shorter than the length of the width of the foam block.

1. Measure the foam block.

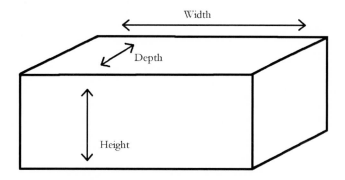

figure A-1 – measuring the foam block

2. Cut 2 pieces of fabric for the ends of the cover. These each need to be the height of the foam block plus 4cm by the depth of the foam block plus 4cm. This gives you a 2cm seam allowance all round.

3. Now cut one piece of fabric that will wrap around the block. This will measure twice the depth by twice the height of the block plus 4cm, and is as wide as the width plus 4cm, again allowing a 2cm seam allowance.

4. Insert a zip along the width edge of your pieces which, when closed, will form a tube of fabric.

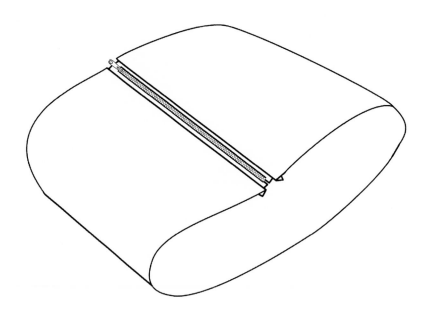

figure A-2 – inserting the zip

5. Turn the tube of fabric inside out. With the right side of the pieces of fabric touching each other and the wrong side outermost, pin and then sew the side pieces to the tube of fabric. Ensure that the zip runs horizontally along the centre of the back of the cushion cover.

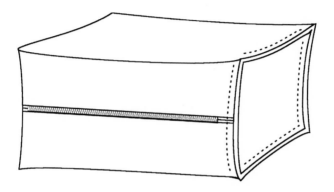

figure A-3 – inserting end pieces of fabric

6. Open the zip and turn the cushion cover the right way out. Insert your foam block into the cover, close the zip and sit on your cushion.

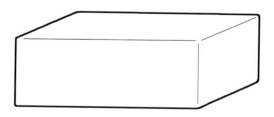

figure A-3 – finished cushion

Appendix B

Round Cushion

These instructions produce a cushion about 16cm high and 26cm in diameter. You will need a piece of fabric at least 150cm long by 60cm wide.

You will need stuffing to fill the cushion, either kapok, buckwheat or beanbag beads.

If a zip is wanted this will be 16cm long.

1. Cut one piece of fabric 20 cm x 150cm, and two circles of fabric 30cm in diameter.

2. On the long rectangular piece of fabric, place a pin 17cm from one edge, and then 12 more pins every following 10cm, so that the last section is 13cm.

3. Make a 2cm pleat at the place of each pin. Fold the first pleat so that it lies on the 17cm edge, and fold all the other pleats in this direction

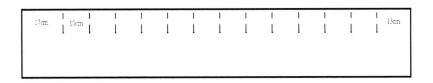

figure B-1 – marking the places for pleats

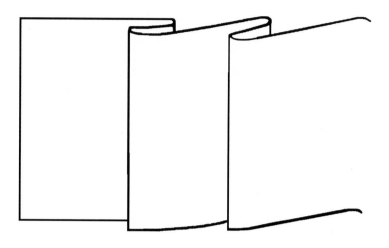

figure B-2 – making the pleats

4. Check this pleated piece is going to fit around the circumference of the fabric circles with an overlap of approximately 2cm each end. If it is a little too long this will not matter. If it is a little too short, adjust the size of the pleats to make it fit. Once you are happy with it, tack along the top and bottom edges to hold the pleats in place and then press the pleats with an iron.

figure B-3 – tacking the pleats

5. Turn in and pin a 2cm hem along each short edge of the pleated piece. Then pin the long edge of the pleated piece around the edge of one of the circles, right side of fabric to right side. The folded back edges of the long pleated piece should butt together – if necessary adjust the depth of hem at each end of the long piece so that they do so. Sew the long pleated piece to the circle.

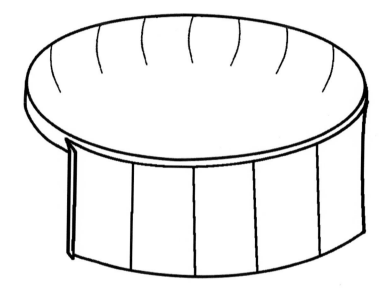

figure B-4 – attaching pleated piece to one circle

6. If you wish to be able to open your cushion to adjust the amount of stuffing, put a zip in at the butted edges of the pleated piece, remembering that it is inside out.

7. Sew the pleated piece onto the second circle in the same way. Remove tacked stitches.

8. Now turn your cushion the right way out through the gap between the sides of the long pleated piece, or by opening the zip if you have inserted one.

9. Stuff the cushion. Each type of stuffing will give a different quality to the feel of the cushion, so you can experiment with this. Kapok will tend to settle after a while and you will need to add more. If you travel a lot with your meditation cushion, you could buy an inflatable ball—such as a beach ball—to put in the cushion cover so that it folds flat for packing and can be inflated for use.

10. Sew up the opening or close the zip and enjoy your sitting practice on your meditation cushion.

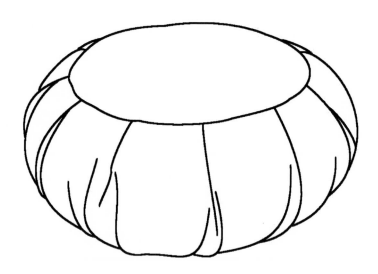

figure B-5 – finished cushion

Appendix C

Flat Cushion

1. Cut two pieces of material 86cm square.

2. If you want a zip in your cushion, insert this first. Fold in a 2cm hem on one side of each square of material and sew the folded edges onto the zip.

figure C-1 – inserting the zip

3. With the right sides of the fabric together, join three sides of the material with a 2cm seam. The fourth side is the one with the zip or is left open at this stage.

figure C-2 – sewing three sides of fabric squares

4. Turn the cushion right side out through the open side (unzip if necessary).

5. Fill the cushion with a piece of foam approximately 5 cm thick, or stuff with kapok or similar filling. Close the zip or neatly sew up the open side.

6. If you are using loose stuffing to fill the cushion, sew a single loop of a strong, thick thread through the cushion in the places illustrated in figure C-3 and tie them in a bow. This will keep the stuffing in place.

figure C-3 – finished cushion with stitches to hold stuffing

Appendix D

Sitting Strap

The materials you will need are strong fabric, such as upholstery cloth and thick interfacing such as buckram. It is quite nice to use a fabric with a pile, such as flocked upholstery cloth, as this will not slip when you wear the strap.

The first thing is to work out the length of your sitting strap. The traditional method of gauging the length is double the measurement from your left ear to the tips of the fingers of your right hand when your arm is stretched out to the side. The measurement for the width is the width of your hand – or approximately 12cm. The width measurement is not so crucial and it can be wider than this, but you do not want it to be narrower or the strap will dig into your skin when sitting.

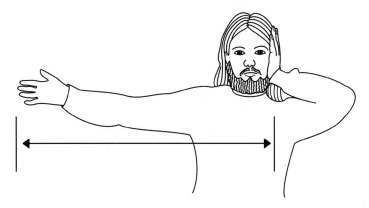

figure D-1 – measuring for the length of meditation strap

1. Cut the fabric to the length and width required, adding a 2cm seam allowance all round.

2. Cut the interfacing to the length and width required – that is without the seam allowance. If it is iron-on interfacing iron it to stick it to the fabric. If not, tack it onto the fabric using a large zigzag pattern of stitching. It should be placed in the centre of the fabric.

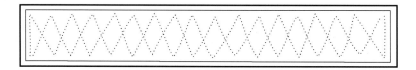

figure D-2 – interfacing

3. Fold the material in half lengthwise, right side to right side, and sew a 2cm seam along the edge to form a narrow tube. Press the tube and the seam open and flat so that the seam lies along the centre rather than at the edge of the fabric.

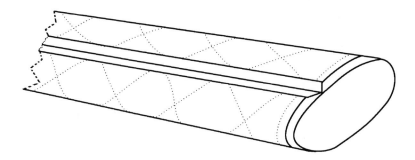

figure D-3 – lengthwise seam

4. Turn the tube right side out.

5. At one end, turn in 2cm of fabric and tack it in place.

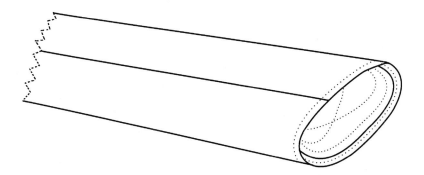

figure D-4 – hem at one end of tube

6. Tuck the end of the fabric tube that does not have the turned-in edge inside the end with the turned-in edge to form a loop of the correct length for the strap and pin in place. Check the length of the strap by sitting with it around your back and knees while still pinned. Once you are sure it is the correct length, over-sew the join several times.

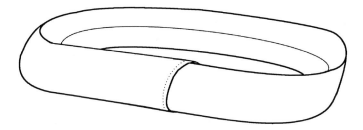

figure D-5 – tuck raw edge of strap into hemmed edge

7. Finally sew a decorative pattern such as a large zigzag design along the length of the strap to attach the back of the strap to the front. This will prevent the fabric becoming twisted when you use it. Remove all tacking.

8. Sit in your meditation strap with it round your knees and lower back.

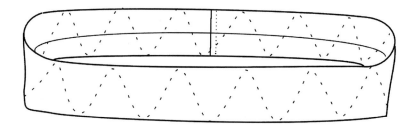

figure D-6 – finished sitting strap

About the Author

Ngakma Nor'dzin's training in meditation began in the early 1980s under the guidance of Tibetan teachers in the UK. She later became a devoted disciple of Ngak'chang Rinpoche and Khandro Déchen. In 1989 she was ordained and became the first Western woman to take ordination into the non-monastic tradition of Nyingma Tibetan Buddhism.

She began teaching classes in community education in 1983, teaching ceramics, homoeopathy, Tibetan yoga, meditation and relaxation. Ngakma Nor'dzin's experience as a Buddhist practitioner and of community education led to the development of the curriculum at the heart of *Relaxing into Meditation*.

Ngakma Nor'dzin grew up in the Midlands of England and moved to Wales as an adult. She now lives in Cardiff with her husband, Ngakpa 'ö-Dzin Tridral, and they have two grown-up sons. From the early years of motherhood she amalgamated her Buddhist training and meditation with family life and work. She and Ngakpa 'ö-Dzin have run a local meditation group for more than twenty years. In the 1990s under the instruction of her teachers, she and Ngakpa 'ö-Dzin started to accept personal students.

Having originally trained in multidisciplinary design, Ngakma Nor'dzin is also a skilled craftswoman and has led several Buddhist craft projects. She has also trained in counselling, reflexology and homoeopathy.

She practises Aro pulse diagnosis and element balancing – a system which promotes individual health and happiness through adjustments to diet and lifestyle.

Her first book, *Spacious Passion*, was published by Aro Books Inc. in 2006 and republished by Aro Books WORLDWIDE in 2009.

Ngakma Nor'dzin has a relaxed style of presentation. She is loved particularly for her warmth and friendliness, her sense of humour and her down-to-earth answers to students' questions. She teaches public events internationally with her husband.

Glossary

A / a

In Tibetan there are two letters with the sound 'A'. To differentiate between them they are often written in western script as a capital *A* and a lower case *a*. The Tibetan syllable *A* is often referred to as the *Dzogchen A* or the primordial *A*. It expresses the simplicity of spontaneous presence of non-dual awareness.

A'a

In Tibetan script, letters can be stacked vertically as well as combined horizontally to form syllables and words. Hence vertical combinations of the two letters that each make the sound 'A' can be used to form separate syllables. *A'a* is a combination of *A* and *a* stacked vertically.

Buddhism

The word 'Buddhism' has been adopted as the word for the religion associated with the teachings of Shakyamuni Buddha. 'Buddha' means 'awakened one' referring to the fact that Shakyamuni awakened and gained realisation. The Sanskrit word for the practice of this religion is 'Dharma' and the Tibetan is 'chö' (*chos*). Buddhism is used as a blanket term to cover the religion, but the Buddhism of the Japanese Zen tradition—for example—is quite different from the Theravadin tradition of Sri Lanka.

community of practitioners

Sanskrit: *sangha*; Tibetan: gendün (*dGe 'dun*).

conceptual mind

Tibetan: sem (*sems*) – the mind that ideates. Thought is a function of conceptual mind.

dharma

Tibetan: chö (*chos*). Literally means *as it is*. The path of practice that leads us to realise the nature of mind.

emptiness

Tibetan: né-pa (*gNas pa*).
The fruit of the practice of *Letting Go*.

equanimity

Tibetan: tang nyom (*bTang sNyoms*).

flat cushion

Zabuton in Japanese.

fundamental mind

Tibetan: sem-nyid (*sems nyid*). *Fundamental mind* or the *nature of mind* is that from which conceptual mind and all the senses arise.

gaze

Gaze has a particular meaning with regard to meditation practice. It is looking, but without expectation of what we might see, and with the possibility of experiencing with all the senses through the sense of sight.

householder tradition

Tibetan: gö kar chang-lo'i dé (*gos dKar lCang lo'i sDe*). The community of non-celibate practitioners who wear white skirts, have long hair, and live ordinary lives as their practice.

knowing

Two aspects of knowing can be identified:
1. knowing through intellectual study and examination,
Tibetan: shérab (*shes rab*); and 2. knowing as primordial
awareness, Tibetan: yeshé (*ye shes*).

letting go

Tibetan: shi-nè (*shi gNas*), Sanskrit: *shamata*. The formless
practice of *Letting Go* is the actual practice of shi-nè. It is
the fundamental practice that leads to the understanding of
the nature of mind. This is explained in depth in the book
'*Roaring Silence*' by Ngakpa Chögyam (Shambala Publications,
2002).

loving kindness

Tibetan: chang chub sem (*byang chub sems*), Sanskrit:
Bodhicitta. At the heart of Tibetan Buddhism is the
Bodhisattva ideal: the extraordinary motivation to engage in
spiritual practice for the benefit of all sentient beings and to
live with valour and integrity.

meditation room

Tibetan: gompa (*sGom pa*).

meditation phenomenon

Tibetan: nyam (*nyams*).

method

Tibetan: Thab (*thabs*), Sanskrit: *upaya*.

mind without thought

Tibetan: né-pa (*gNas pa*) – the fruit of the practice of shi-nè
(*Letting Go*).

nature of mind

Tibetan: sem nyi (*sems nyid*). The fundamental state of mind which can be discovered through meditation. It is not conditioned by thoughts, opinions and neurosis.

ngakma

Tibetan: ngakma (*sNgags ma*) – pronounced 'nak-ma'. The title for a woman who has taken ordination in the gö kar chang-lo'i dé (*gos dKar lCang lo'i sDe*) – literally 'mantra woman'. The male equivalent is Ngakpa.

neurosis

Tibetan: nyon mong (*nyon mongs*) The duality of holding to the form qualities of solidity, permanence, separation, continuity and definition; while denying the empty qualities of lack of solidity, impermanence, inseparability, discontinuity and lack of definition. This five-fold expression of neurotic patterning relates to the five elements earth, water, fire, air and space. The form qualities of the elements exist *in the moment*, but do not continue unchanged from moment to moment.

Nyingma

The most ancient of the four schools of Buddhism in Tibet.

Om, A'a Hung

The primary function of these syllable is in the practice of Tantra to refer to the non-dual state of mind, voice and body, or emptiness, energy and form.

presence

This is the state of being completely aware and alert in the present moment – being aware of all that is arising in the mind and the sense fields, or being peacefully alert if nothing is arising. It is a state of vibrant, relaxed openness.

rectangular cushion

Gomden in Tibetan. This style of meditation cushion was first introduced by Chögyam Trungpa Rinpoche the founder of Shambala Training. 'Gomden' is a registered trade mark of Vajradhatu and these cushions are available to purchase from Samadhi Cushions.

round cushion

Zafu in Japanese.

rhythm breathing

A preliminary exercise for the practice of tumo (*gTum mo* – inner heat). The practice of generating inner heat through meditation and physical practice and control of the breath. In this book it is used as a simple breathing exercise.

sitting strap

Tibetan: gomtag (*sGom thag*).

song

There are two types of meditational song in the Tibetan tradition: dön-pa (*'don pa*) and yang (*dByangs*). Dön-pa, or chant, focuses on the meaning of the words as the principle of the practice. In yang it is the experience of singing itself that is the focus of the practice.

song leader

Tibetan: um-dzé (*dbU mDzad*).

teacher

Tibetan: Lama (*bLa ma*) – the title used for experienced and learned teachers of Buddhism, who through study, practice, and devotion to their own teachers and lineage are able to teach and transmit Dharma.

thunderbolt sceptre

Tibetan: dorje (*rDo rJe*), Sanskrit: *vajra*.

Tibetan yoga

sKu-mNyé (*sKu mNye*).

transformation

In Tibetan Buddhism the teachings are presented from different perspectives called vehicles (Tibetan: thegpa – *theg pa;* Sanskrit: *yana*). The delineation of vehicles varies from tradition to tradition. Tantra is the vehicle of transformation in terms of allowing ourselves to use our emotions and circumstances as an aspect of our practice.

Index